Crooked Lines

An Autobiography
By
Freda Hicks

For my grandchildren
With love...

'Wealth may be courted,
Wisdom revered,
And beauty praised,
And brutal strength feared,
But goodness can only affection move,
And Love must owe its origin to Love.'

Freda Hicks 1978

PART ONE

CHAPTER 1

The thirteen-year-old boy at the back of the class was being particularly unbearable. Others around him were joining in and making me wonder what on earth I was doing, trying to teach such unruly monsters when I could be taking it relatively easy at home just looking after my husband and schoolboy son.

My face blazing with anger I strode towards the boy who was the ringleader, grabbed him fiercely by the shoulders, and shook him with all my strength.
"Who do you think you are?" I bellowed. And then again, shaking him all the time with each word coming out almost as a gasp as I rocked him to and fro,
"Who - do- you - think - you - are?"

There was a shocked silence in the room for I had never behaved in this way before and must have given the impression that I was experiencing a brain storm, so enraged was I for those few moments. The boy straightened himself in his desk, swallowed, looked me with utter hopelessness and said gruffly,
"I dunno 'oo I be. A 'uman bein' I s'pose.'

My heart was beating like a sledgehammer against my ribs and my legs felt like jelly as I snapped,
"Well act like one then."

But his words had shaken me for they seemed to say so much and I felt ashamed that I had made such an exhibition of myself. And that is how it all started, because after this incident I began to take a really hard look at myself, and the thought that kept repeating itself in my mind was who did I think I was, losing my temper like that and behaving in such an unseemly manner?

****

I was forty-five when I first walked through the gates of Pennygillam Secondary Modern, a Cornish school accommodating pupils from a very wide country area. After a break from teaching of several years I had been helping out in local primary schools during teachers' absences and as I lived near the District Education Officer it was easy for him to get in touch with me quickly and send me off to fill in as a temporary teacher.

But I was not very keen to fill in at Pennygillam. I was used to teaching juniors, and anyway, I had heard dreadful tales about the Secondary Modern. It was reputed to be 'awful' and "a dump' and I had often heard it said that nobody in the right senses would go there to teach. So, when the Education Officer asked me if I could help him out yet again I began to hedge but could think of no real reason why I should let him down.

"It's only for a couple of weeks," he said hopefully, "and all you have to do is take the backward children for a bit of reading and writing."

The regular part-time teacher's husband was very ill but over the worst, and she would soon be back to take up her normal duties once more. That was his version anyway.

"Well," I thought, "It's not for very long and will add up to experience."

So, on a well-remembered September afternoon I set off to meet this new challenge - ten half-days only of teaching 'a bit of reading and writing to backward children.' Or so I thought...

The boys and girls awaiting afternoon school looked enormous after those I had been used to teaching. And yes, rough too some of them, like people has said. But most of them looked no different to those at the grammar school and I began to take heart as I made my way to the staff room to meet the senior mistress. I had already been to see the regular teacher who had briefed me on the kind of work I should be expected to do. It was now a matter of getting my timetable and putting it into operation.

The piece of paper I was given seemed to be a jumbled maze of numbers and letters with classroom allocation alongside. 1C, 2C, 1B, 2Bs, 3C, and the various other combinations floated before my eyes, and the letter C was the one most in evidence. These groups turned out to be the less able children, and me, Heaven help me was there to teach them....

The bell went, and with it so did my heart. My head was in a whirl. Whatever had made me decide to come to this school? How was I going to cope? Could I back out even at this late stage? 'Roll on the next fortnight," was my predominant thought as the senior mistress took me to meet my first class which was 1C. Thank goodness they were not bigger than me, anyway. They eyed me suspiciously. Some lived near me and knew my quite well. They had probably never thought of me as a teacher of older children, and yet there I was having the cheek to think that I could teach them.

As it happened they turned out to be very well behaved that afternoon and I marvelled at the way they accepted their lot. And that 'lot' was not very much....

The school consisted of buildings that were remnants of the Second World War. The site had once housed an army camp and until a new school could be built was considered suitable as temporary buildings for the eleven to fifteen year-olds who had not passed the eleven-plus examination. The science laboratory was a Nissen hut as was the assembly hall and dining room. Other classrooms were more 'refined' but quite obviously just make-do huts. They did not look too bad from outside but were very drab inside. Gas fires spluttered fitfully on the walls ad in the winter the concrete floors were forever wet.

I am of the opinion that a good education does not depend on fine buildings, carpets, curtains and the like and have often heard it said that a good teacher could get good results operating from a wheelchair in a tent provided sufficient books were available. Pennygillam School was not ideal in many respects and had many excellent teachers - teachers who transformed their drab surroundings into places of interest with stimulating materials and wall displays.

Many of the pupils did very well indeed, going on to places of further education and taking up academic careers. Those with less scholastic ability but skilled in practical work also left school and did well, but it was evident form the start that the children with general learning difficulties were not getting a fair deal. They seemed to be housed out of sight as far as possible and were the troublemakers, many of them. But it was not surprising really. Some teachers regarded them as of no importance and they acted accordingly. They were 'duffers' or 'cretins' according to some of the less understanding teachers and suffered all kinds of verbal abuse.

The pupils were never in on e room all the time. There was a great deal of moving about from one classroom to another and this was the part of secondary education that I found most irritating at first. In one afternoon it was quite usual to teach in three different buildings and when the rain was pouring down it became very trying indeed for pupils and staff alike. I became a sort of walking teachers' desk bearing my pencils and rulers and other equipment that never seemed adequate, from one place to another.

I did not enjoy those first ten half days. 3C turned out to be very different to 1C. These were the pupils who had worked out that they were never likely to be any good at bookwork. Nobody seemed to care much about them and they didn't care either. It was a small, difficult class and when I first met them, they were grouped together at the back of the room, mostly boys who even when sitting down, looked like young giants. I felt like an animal trainer venturing into a cage of vicious tigers. I could almost imagine them baring their teeth and snarling at my approach. It was as if they were saying, "You dare to try and teach us anything and we'll make your life a misery."

So, I didn't try. Not that first time anyway. We talked. Or rather, they did. I listened to all they had to say although it was difficult at times as they all wanted to be talking at once, sort of getting it out of their systems and, of course, in their minds, craftily avoiding work.

They could not read very well so it followed that they could not easily write much out of their own heads - only from a copy. They covered up their lack of ability by insisting that they did not need reading and certainly they saw no necessity for being able to write.
"What do us want to read for? There's flicks."
"Us don't want to write to anybody. What's the telephone for?"
"What time do us 'ave for reading and writing after us get 'ome?"

It appeared that they had to work at home, and very hard some of them. Farm animals had to be fed, sheds had to be cleaned, cars and tractors had to be looked after. There were other more important things than book learning.
"It's all a waste of time," was how they summed it up, but by my reckoning they desperately wanted to learn the basic skills

of reading and writing and all the reasons they were giving for their unimportance was sheer bravado.

So, what to do? They were not going to settle down happily to much schoolwork. They had made that plain. I felt helpless and longed for my teaching stint to come to an end. But it went on, and on, and on....

The sick husband did not improve and his illness was to stretch over many months. Mr. Insley, the kindly head teacher, told me that I 'fitted in', and from asking me if I could 'come back next month' went on to, "You'll come back next term, won't you?" And then another... and another. I could see no end to it but I struggled on. It seemed to me that I was not doing very well but I took the work seriously and did my best.

There were other teachers as well as myself engaged in caring for the less able in the basic subjects. There were the mornings to be timetabled and there were other important subjects as well as the three R's. Some of the teachers were good while others were unbelievably bad. One of them had no control whatsoever. During her lessons there was absolute chaos; paper darts flew around and the noise was unbearable. Once in total despair she just let them get on with 'their fun' while she busied herself with her knitting. She was very young and inexperienced and it must have been soul-destroying to find herself in such a situation.

Over the years the good teachers of the weaker brethren had come and gone, to move on to other schools, to get married, or because of pregnancy. Except for the fourth year teachers they were usually women who were landed with the slow learners, especially while I was there, and this coming and going resulted in a lack of continuity in the work of the pupils who needed stability above all.

It was some time after that troublesome boy had unknowingly made me ask myself who I thought I was that I really began to get myself together. I should not have bellowed at him; I certainly should not have lost my temper. This was no way to deal with pupils who had learning difficulties. They needed love and understanding and a finely programmed learning scheme to help them find their way. It was no good hoping for the best without striving for it.

It was clear that if I wished, I could stay on at the school for there was a shortage of teachers at that time. By now we knew that the regular teacher would definitely not be returning, but this did not mean I had to carry on. Why not throw in the towel? The work was so demanding that even after only part-time work I found myself whacked by the evening and often emotionally drained. But then I was beginning to love the 'little hellers' as the children were sometimes called, and even the young giants that I had once feared and screamed at now had a place in my heart. The Headmaster was right. I did fit in, for I was not a brilliant academic, too clever to understand the workings of ordinary brains, and it was not hard for me to get down to the level of the slow learners.

Who did I think I was? I wasn't even a qualified teacher but at least I knew I was working the right direction. I was building up a good relationship with my pupils, for by now they knew that in spite of my earlier 'stumblings' I was on their side. I talked to them in their own language and told them of my own struggles at school and at home. But through it all there had always been someone I could lean on. I suppose I could have been called an underprivileged child, though all things considered I was certainly not a deprived one, but because of the help I had received during my school days I have become a very privileged adult indeed.

Yes. That is what I was, a very privileged human being. And I had it in me to be of use to the underprivileged because I had not had things easy either, and we could identify with each other.... The pieces of my life were falling into place to shape what was to be, as far as I was concerned, complete fulfilment. My daughter was about to get married, my son no longer needed me at home all the time, and I certainly wanted something more than the routine existence of a housewife. Here was a challenge that could broaden my life and give me the satisfaction of doing something really worthwhile. My husband was all for it too for he understood me well.

I told the Headmaster that I would stay....

Chapter 2

My father died in 1923 when I was seven, the eldest of three children. My brother was five and my sister three. If my father had lived, things would have been very different and we would not have had to endure the poverty that we all knew until we could stand on our own two feet.

William Oldridge, forth from the right at Castle Green stall

I do not remember much about my father himself, but certain childhood memories remain vivid in my mind. He was a plumber who owned his own business and had two men working for him, and exalted position indeed in those days. Things were going well but housing was a problem and we lived in two rooms. All my early childhood was spent living in part of someone else's house. The most remembered items of furniture were the large double beds with enormous brass knobs on the iron framework. I remember them because we always hung our stockings on the tall bedrails at Christmas and the knobs glistened magically in the candlelight as we eagerly got between the sheets. There were no interior sprung mattresses then but huge 'ties' as they were called, filled with feathers, enveloped our small bodies and were warm and comfortable.

There were two of these beds in our one small bedroom and not much room for anything else. Our parents slept in one of them and the three children in the other. We could not lie side by side as we grew bigger and so one of us had always to sleep at the bottom of the bed, the wrong way round as it were.

My father's Christian name was Oldridge but for some unknown reason he was known to almost everyone as Fogie. He was a great one for taking part in the carnival held each year to help the local hospital and arranged as near to Guy

Fawkes Day as possible, thus brightening up the dreary month of November. The Carnival was the event of the year with its torch-lit procession wending its way through the narrow streets of our small Cornish town, a splendid parade of walking guys and tableaux headed by mounted horses and the Town Band bringing a magical quality to the whole affair.

The gas-lit streets were lined with people who had waited patiently in the cold evening air for the procession to start. They came from nearby towns and villages and the collecting tins were very much in evidence, carried usually by well-known characters in weird attires and causing great amusement.

People prepared their tableaux weeks in advance of the carnival and I have a picture in my mind of my father, as the day drew nearer, blowing up hundreds of balloons to decorate a horse-drawn wagon labelled, 'Every Copper Helps'. He was dressed as a policeman and it was not a prize he was after as a fine collection of pennies for the hospital. Another year he produced 'Pip, Squeak and Wilfred' and what I remember most about this year was the goat tethered on the wagon and selling to high heaven. 'Good old Fogie' was the cry.
S'M '\

But best of all was the burning house. My father belonged to the fire brigade and with the help of other firemen constructed

15

a huge cardboard house to be towed around the streets on a wagon. He had managed to get smoke pouring realistically from the building and my sister and I, in our nightdresses, were being lifted to safety through the windows. We were very young at the time, appealing little souls evoking the sympathy of the crowds as we rattled perilously by. The smoke was getting into our eyes and almost choking us too, but I suppose it made it all the more dramatic and we were awarded Third Prize. People in the town still talk of the carnivals of long ago and of Fogie who played such an important part in them. They left a considerable impression on my mind for whenever I come across a photograph of my father my mind always switches to those wonderful processions of long ago.

It is strange how certain smells bring back memories. As well as the goat in the carnival I remember the smell of my father's greyhounds and ferrets. Not that the dogs were ever used for racing, but with the help of the ferrets, kept in a small yard outside where we lived, they did manage to catch a few rabbits which made delicious pies that went down really well when they were cold and the pink flesh was enclosed in savoury jelly. The ferrets were vicious little creatures with pink eyes that terrified me and sometimes I would be invited to touch one of these cream-coloured streaks of fur, but I never would. Goodness knows where the greyhounds were kept;

there was certainly no room for them in the house. They looked so thin and always appeared to be trembling with excitement. I hated them for they were not a bit cuddly and there was always their smell, especially when they were wet after a day in the fields.

Sometimes my father took us fishing. This was such an adventure, going to the nearby wood and wending our way along the riverbank after having collected flies from the accommodating cowpats in the fields. Not that we ever caught many fish, but a spotted trout wriggling on the ground was an awesome sight and even one as young as I could not fail to be moved by the wonderful markings on its body and saddened to see it struggling in its death throes.

My father's work often took him into the surrounding countryside. He would hire a pony and trap and as a special treat I was allowed to go with him, in turn with my brother and sister. It often meant long waits outside country houses in which he worked but it was all such an adventure and so exciting.

The roads were very rough in those days and country lanes worse still, but the pony's hooves clattering on the stones was music to my ears, and the trap, or jingle as it was sometimes called, a thing of great delight with its brass fittings and shiny wooden seats. Sometimes we met the veterinary surgeon on his rounds. He had a fine jingle of his own and must have travelled around the countryside in this way for miles and miles, flicking his whip and smiling graciously at the people he met as he travelled along.

And then my father became very ill....

By this time we had moved into two rooms in my grandmother's house along with several other relatives. There was a large shed suitable as a base for a plumber at the back of the building and it was more convenient for my father to live in close proximity to his workshop. It did not please my mother for she never did get on with her in-laws, and least of all with granny who was very much the boss. It must have been very difficult sharing a kitchen in these circumstances and worse still when illness struck.

My father had pneumonia, a dreadful disease in the 1920s when there were no curative drugs available and houses were overcrowded. He was so ill that soft wood chippings were strew over the road outside so that horse-drawn carriages would not make so much noise as they passed by. The doctor was a regular visitor and we all had to be very quiet. The house was full of children for my father's sister also lived in the house with her three children and there were always other cousins around as well.

Granny Body's grandsons outside Westgate street house

I do not remember much about my mother at this time, only that she wore pince-nez spectacles which showed ugly marks on the sides of her nose when she took them off to wipe away the tears. It was my aunt who had come from London who told us that our father had died during the night and that we would all have to be very brave. My brother and sister were obviously too young to understand, and mercifully, I did not fully understand the significance of all that was happening.

It was a big funeral because my father was so well known and respected. I stood at the window of that old house and watched the comings and goings on that sad day. As each relative entered our one room and embraced my mother she burst into a flood of tears asking desperately,

"What be I be goin' to do?" This was repeated over and over again. She was not yet twenty-seven and now found herself a widow with three young children to care for. What indeed was she going to do?

The hearse drew up outside the house and the coffin was placed inside with my father's fireman's helmet and tools on the top. And that is all I remember about it except that smell of the hyacinths and other early spring flowers that seemed to hang around the house long after the wreaths were removed. It is a smell that to this day, I always associate with funerals.

We were too young to go to the funeral so a neighbour's daughter took the three of us, complete with black armbands, for a walk to get us out of the way. People stopped to talk to us and everybody appeared to be very kind. The looks on their faces and their hushed voices told me something dreadful had happened in our lives. No more rides into the countryside or adventures by the river... and there was our mother who seemed to have been crying ever since my father became ill and never took any notice of us at all.
"Poor little souls," people said. "Whatever will become of them?"

I had heard of other poor fatherless children and **they** had ended up in The Workhouse. I listened to the relatives talking about my mother's circumstances and something about not stamping a card. It appeared that because my father was, to use their own words 'his own boss' he had not stamped an insurance card, which meant that my mother could not draw a widow's pension. Indeed, from now on she would have to rely upon what she herself could earn and upon charity....

'Faith, Hope and Charity'. How often had I heard those words as a child. And how did it go on? 'And the greatest of these is Charity'. But nobody really wanted to live on charity. That was a different thing altogether. People had their pride and it was considered a disgrace to have to resort to it.

But sometimes there is no other way....

Chapter 3

My mother was a little slip of a woman who was destined to now nothing much except hard work for most of her life. She had married during the war just before my father went off to France and when she was obviously too young to know her own mind. The in-laws disapproved her from the very beginning and there were often scenes between my parents because of this. Sometimes, as I lay at night pretending to be asleep in the adjoining bed, I could hear them airing their grievances against one another, my mother usually ending up in a tearful rage and threatening to run away from it all.

She was described as being flighty and irresponsible and as they years went by I realised that she was certainly no angel. Her name was Lily, a very inappropriate name, all things considered, but she was always full of pluck and knew how to stand up for herself and her children.

We lived in my grandmother's house for about five years after my father died and in spite of the constant bickering which went on between my mother and her in-laws, it was to me a place of refuge. It was in Westgate Street, a semi-detached house near the town centre. The door opened straight on to the pavement to all and sundry. Relatives and friends were always popping to call on granny and miraculously there was always a cup of tea at hand. The teapot was very large and covered by an ancient tea-cosy that appeared to have no colour except that of the tea stains which had been there for many years. There was a smell about it that was homely and comforting.

My grandmother was a dressmaker and had lived in that house for most of her life so far. She was proud of the way that she had learned her trade and become accomplished enough to have her own apprentices in her younger days. So one of the rooms in the house was always known as the workroom.

There were two main rooms at street level, the one my family had, and the workroom in which the other members of that crowded house lived. Along a dark passage and down some worn steps was the kitchen that seemed always to be full of people. In one corner was a worn sink, with a tap that never stopped hissing. You would never have guessed that a plumber had once lived in the house!

The family had a horror of draughts so an ancient screen covered the back door that was seldom used. The screen was rather like the tea-copy in that it had a smell of its own having stood so long in that airless kitchen and it was decorated with old pictures that had been cut out of various books over the years.

The three bedrooms were overcrowded to say the least. Granny had her own small room but sometimes shared it with other members of the family especially when relatives from London came for their holidays. The other two bedrooms were occupied by my mother and her three children in one and my Auntie Mabel and her three in the other. Then, when her husband came on leave form the navy that made one more, and as a result of one of his leaves, another baby was on the way. We could all be squeezed in like sardines in a time and still not be disturbed during the night when my aunt's fourth son was born. We woke in the morning and there he was. "The nurse brought him," we were told.

As well as the three bedrooms there were two small attic rooms. In one lived a very old veterinary surgeon. He was incredibly ancient, as wrinkled as a prune, but he was very dignified and clever and filled me with awe especially as he was not just a plain old mister, but a doctor! He smoked a clay pipe as he sat on the windowsill outside the house and chatted to people as they passed by. Sometimes we used to blow bubbles with his discarded pipes, and that this was a very undesirable practice as regards hygiene never entered anyone's head, but happily we suffered no ill effects.

Auntie Min slept in the other attic room. She was an old lady and how she managed to climb those rickety old stairs up top her room remains a mystery. The attic ceiling slanted almost to the floor and there was just enough room to squeeze in her single bed and small dressing table. I was not allowed in Dr. Philp's room but often went into the other attic room. It was very strange up there and smelled of all things old in spite of the fresh smell of eau-de-Cologne and sweet oil that were always on the dressing table.

The house was very old, one of the oldest in the town. The downstairs rooms had stone floors that were like the waves of the sea and the walls seemed to bulge all over; I never remember them being re-coloured or repapered. Lying in bed we used to count the roses on the faded paper and look for patterns in the cracks on the ceiling. On one occasion, however, the front door and the stairs were treated to a face-lift. One of my uncles was a painter and decorator and he came to do some graining. I was fascinated as I watched him skillfully combing the still wet coat of paint to give it an effect of wood-grain that was very fine indeed. When he had finished, the door was undoubtedly the best in the street with its shiny surface and heavy brass knocker that was polished every day.

The walls of the house were hung with antiquated pictures, mostly texts telling us that the Lord was our shepherd or that angels were watching over us. We believed it too for Granny and Auntie Min were always telling us that God would look after us.

The house was lit by gas lamps, but only in the downstairs rooms. The meter was in the coalhouse under the stairs - what a performance it was when the lights went out and the necessary coin had to be found.

But it really was a case of 'Here comes the candle to light you to bed' for anything else would have been unheard of luxury. It is incredible that all four of my cousins living in that house had, to my certain knowledge, been born by candlelight, and probably my mother's three as well.

There was no hot water system in the house. Every drop of water had to be boiled in a kettle on the workroom fire or on the old black range in the kitchen. Washday was a major operation. The clothes were washed in large galvanised baths placed on the scrubbed kitchen tale and a neighbour used to come in to help wash, blue and starch the clothes which were then put through the huge wooden rollers of a squeaky old mangle.

If washday was a major operation, I don't know what you would call bath night. One of the washing baths would be filled with water, carried to the living room and placed before the fire. What with the uneven passage floor and awkward doorways it could not be done without splashing out a great deal of the water along the way. Then, having gone through all the soaping and swilling of our young bodies, my mother had to return the bath water to the kitchen, no easy task in the winter without lights along the way.

But in the workroom, all was peace and tranquility. No matter how many visitors came to that place there was always a seat for everyone. The walls of the house were bulging already but relatives would come from London each summer and squeeze in with all of us; we all fitted in somehow.

Granny continued with her dress making and as well as serving as a dining-come-living room filled with furniture the workroom housed two sewing machines, numerous boxes of cotton and pins and needles and a tailor's dummy which did not look at all out of place amongst us all and was almost a part of the family.

Bits of cloth and cotton, or 'triffles' as granny called them, littered the floor on most days, but certainly not Sundays, and partly finished garments hung at various points around the room. Some days the flat iron would come out, to be heated on the fire and used to press garments under a damp cloth. How I loved the sizzling and the smell of the cloth as Granny's bony hands manoeuvred the iron over the garments that she had so expertly fashioned.

But for all the activity that went on in the workroom, and however many of us were squeezed in there, it was always a place where I felt secure and loved. And although it must have been chaotic I never remember it as being orderly and peaceful. Although we had our own living room I spent a lot of time in the workroom. If I had used my eyes and really watched Granny's deft fingers I may have become an expert dressmaker as my sister turned out to be, but I was a bit of a dreamer and looked without really seeing.

I was a sensitive little soul though and watched with pity as the flies got trapped on the sticky flypapers that hung from the ceiling in the summer. There was also a glass contraption containing sweetened vinegar that trapped the flies and left them swimming helplessly in the vile looking liquid. The all struck me as being cruel but Granny said that she had to keep the flies down as they marked the garments. It is difficult to understand how they got into the house in the first place for the windows were rarely opened. They did not believe in fresh air in that house so they must have some through the door with all the other visitors!

My memory is probably playing tricks with me. I loved that room with all its busy smells but when I consider its size and all the furniture therein, and the number of people always there at one time, and the stained tea cosy, the fly papers, and the singeing cloth under the hot iron, and the gaslight, and the smell of food in the cupboards, and the great age of some of the room's occupants and their hatred of fresh air, I think it must have been very much like a scene out of Dickens. But it played a very important part in my life and I remember it with love and gratitude. In that room Granny fashioned many fine garments, and in her way I think she played a large part in fashioning me: frayed edges and all!

Chapter 3

My mother and grandmother did not speak to each other. The enmity between them lasted for as long as I can remember and was difficult for me to understand at the time. In my mother's eyes the old lady was an interfering old busybody but in mine she was always what other people in Launceston later called her, Launceston's Grand Old Lady.

Mary Body was born in Jersey where her father John Vosper, a member of an old Launceston Family, had gone for a short time, but she returned to Cornwall at an early age to set up her own dressmaking business at the age of twenty two, continuing with it until she was almost ninety. She was proud of her ancestry and of the Vosper crest that bore the words, 'Utraque, Fortuna, Contentus' (gleaned from the Vosper family tree but surely not authentic)!

She was the mother of four sons and three daughters and around the time that my father died had several grandchildren. The family grew considerably as time went by and she ended up with fifteen grandchildren and twelve great grandchildren. She was well and truly head of the family and reigned like a queen. It was true that she interfered but when she said that she knew best, and we did not always believe it, it usually turned out that she knew what she was talking about.

Granny (Mary) Body

She had been a window for many years and from my earliest recollections she was a very old lady. I always remember her in black with touches of white and she wore her clothes with a flair for fashion and with great dignity. She seldom went out anywhere and when she did it was an event, either going to church or carrying flowers to her husband's grave in the cemetery about a mile away. She was an upright figure, her skirt reaching almost to the ground as she walked regally around. Her black hat boasted a large ostrich feather and, scorning a walking stick, she usually carried a parasol with a long handle.

But the thing that I remember most was the narrow band of black velvet that she wore around her neck. It seemed to be a fixture and I wondered if she ever took it off. I don't suppose she ever had a bath in her later years and looking back, I wonder where she carried out her toilet for I do not remember any such facilities in her bedroom. She used to say,
"I wash down as far as possible and up as far as possible," and then she would say, with a twinkle in her eye, "So it looks as if poor old possible never gets washed at all!"

So there doesn't seem to be much to be said in favour of hygiene and fresh air considering she lived to be one hundred and one, and her mother before her, in the same house, to ninety-six. Maybe Granny's old age could be contributed to the fact that she refused to worry about anything. Or it could be the jug of ale she fetched form the public house opposite every evening except Sundays for as long as I can remember.

Goodness knows she had plenty to worry about. All four of her sons were in France during the First World War but she put her trust in God. She always said,

"What will be, will be. And whatever happens, God knows best." Months would go by without news of her sons but she told us how she went to church and prayed for their safety and then left it all in God's hands. And when they all came back safely, she did not forget to go to church and thank God that He had seen fit to spare them.

There were times when she had not a penny in the house, but according to her, 'God would provide" and sure enough one of her customers would be at the door to pay for work she had done.

"It's no good to worry about anything," she would tell us, "Not if you can't do anything about it." I wish I could have followed her example but some people worry and others do not, and there is nothing you can do about that either.

I wonder what she thought when my father died leaving three small children and a wife she did not consider competent to look after them. She never shed a tear at that time, nor did she several years later when another son and not long after a daughter, died of cancer after much suffering. That she loved us all, there can be no doubt, but she showed this in practical ways and not with kisses and cuddles. She was not demonstrative in this way but she told me long after I was grown up that when my father died she had one ambition, and that was to live long enough to see her fatherless grandchildren successfully reared.

It may have been God's will that this ambition should be realised but she herself had to give Him a hand. Not only did she live to see us on our own feet, but with time to spare as well. Indeed, when she was over ninety it was I who presented her with her first great grandchild. And yes, it was then for the very first time that I saw a tear glistening on her wizened cheeks.

Granny Body in her nineties with first granddaughter, Andrea

Chapter 5

Obviously, it was my mother who faced the hardest task when it came to rearing her young family. As there was no widow's pension for her she had to seek help from other sources. So we 'went on the Parish' a very odd way of putting it I must say. What it really meant was that my mother had to go to the church schoolroom each week, along with other poor unfortunates in the town, to pick up her Parish Pay. I believe it came out of the rates and was administered by the Board of Guardians. Anyway, when I was older I was sometimes reminded by my catty 'friends' at school that their parents helped to keep us.

It amounted to one pound per week and it never changed until we all finally left school and it was stopped. Prices were very stable in those days and the word 'inflation' was never heard, and a good thing too! But a pound did not go very far so my mother had to go out to work, a comedown for any married woman at the time.

She had left school as soon as she was fourteen and gone into domestic service. In other words she had been a skivvy and would have to go back into that kind of work again. She worked very hard for eight pence (old money) an hour and in one house where she slaved her wages were reduced if she had a cup of tea and a biscuit in the morning. Her employer was quite well off and called herself a Christian....

It was a credit to that frail little woman who was my mother that we never went hungry. Meals were not very varied and must have been prepared under very trying circumstances indeed. I do not think there is a woman alive who really enjoys sharing a kitchen, and certainly not one where there is not just one other woman but three, and not very well liked at that. But, for all the disharmony, not one of them ever said a word to us children against our mother. Indeed I have the suspicion that as time went by, Granny even admired her in a way, and would have liked a better relationship between them.

A lot of our meals were prepared on the single gas ring in our living room, or on the fire that we had in the winter months. We had boiled smoked haddock because it was fairly cheap and did not take long to cook, and endless bowls of Oxo broth. Oxtail was relatively cheap too and made good soup. With the addition of split peas you could almost stand up a spoon in it, it was so thick and filling. Sometimes for breakfast we had kettle broth that was simply a hunk of bread broken up into a basin with boiling water poured over it. The addition of a knob of butter and pepper and salt made a warming meal if rather a watery one.

We ate a great deal of lettuce in the summer months, chopped up and swimming in vinegar. We had never heard of salad cream and anything out of a tin was regarded as rubbish. But most of all I remember the soaked crusts. The crusts of bread were put into a large basin and tea poured over them through a strainer. A saucer was then placed on top of the basin to keep the heat in and to allow the tea to soak into the crusts and soften them. We ate the resulting 'sog' with syrup or jam on the top and, if we were lucky, a spoonful of cream as well. That was real luxury!

How I loved fetching the Sunday cream. I carried the small ornamental dish to the shop where it was weighed. The cream was then taken from a huge bowl of milk that had been slowly heated and left to cool until a delicious crust had formed over the top. The shopkeeper would scoop some of this marvellous stuff off and into the dish. Sometimes I would ask proudly for a quarter of cream but often we could only afford two ounces. A piece of greaseproof paper was put over the top and as I carried it home it was too much of a temptation and I could not resist poking my finger into it for a furtive lick and then smoothing the top over again so that nobody would know. When the dish was emptied at teatime, but there were still some bits left sticking to the sides, we took it in turns to lick it out.

We had to take turns for lots of things. A rabbit was a good buy, much cheaper than beef, and a variety of meals could be prepared from it. There was roast rabbit with breadcrumbs and onions baked crisply on the top, rabbit pie, and easiest of all on the gas ring, rabbit stew. But there were only two kidneys that we all enjoyed, so we had to work out a rota for these. Nobody wanted the ribs. They were so bony with little flesh on them, but if we didn't have a rib one week, we'd have it the next. It was a case of,

"Whose turn is it for the waistcoats?"

There was no such thing as school milk. Nor did we ever see it in bottles in those days. The milk cart used to come round with the milk in huge churns. You could have new milk or skimmed which was cheaper. The latter was what had been made for making cream and was what we usually had. It was dipped out with measures and transferred to the waiting jugs. I don't suppose the milk cart was very clean, and the patient horse pulling it seemed to attract a great many flies during the summer. Nobody had heard of pasturised or tuberculin tested milk, but although I for one did not grow fat, at least we seldom required a doctor. We had the usual illnesses like chickenpox and measles but bounced back to health very quickly.

Fish was also brought around in a cart, also horse-drawn. In season you could buy enough herrings to make a good meal for a few pence. When we were eating them we were told to be careful not to eat the swimmer, a small silvery organ of the fish near the backbone. I did not know which part of the fish this was or why we should not eat it but we were always eager to see whether we had a soft or a hard roe because we each had our favourite and often do a swap if we had the wrong one.

We drank cocoa for breakfast and supper. It was more nourishing than coffee and anyway that was very special and you could only have a sniff at it at church socials and Christmas suppers in the church hall, and what a delicious aroma.

We could not be choosy with our food. After all there were two hundred and forty pence in a pound when we were children and at eight pence an hour my mother had to work for thirty hours to get another pound to supplement her Parish Pay. Sometimes she did a hard day's work for just three-shillings which we spent on food the very day she received it, so she could not afford to waste anything. We ate what was placed in front of us and if we did not, then it was kept back for us to eat at the next meal.

Sometimes we were allowed the luxury of sweets, especially if uncles or aunts were visiting and we were given a few coppers. It was sheer joy to go to the shop on the corner near our house to choose the sweets from the many glass jars lined up on the shelves. There were no automatic weighing machines then, but the balance type scales which were used with brass weights. A pennyworth of sweets was something to be cherished and I would never eat them all at once. They were carefully weighed by the shopkeeper who would not dream of putting one extra into the triangular shaped paper bag. Often I would ask for two separate 'happorths' as it seemed I got more that way.

If we had hard-boiled sweets we were not allowed to grind them up in our mouths but were told to suck them slowly. It was not that our mother was concerned about our teeth but she couldn't bear the noise!
"For God's sake stop grinding they sweets," she would say crossly, "They set my teeth on edge!"

We knew when we were spoken to and our mother's little whims.
"Take your feet of the bar of the chair," she would order. Or, "Take your elbows off the table," when we were having our meals. We were not naughty children but undoubtedly we frequently got o' her nerves. She often said she didn't know

why people had 'chullern'. If they came along by accident, well then you had to put up with them, but to deliberately go in for a family? Well, that was beyond her comprehension.

Normally there were seven children in the house but is my memory playing tricks on me, or did youngsters scream less in those days?   It seems that nowadays children are not enjoying themselves unless they are screaming enough to burst their lungs. We were always being told as children that we should be seen and not heard so I think that such noise as screaming was out as far as we were concerned, especially in the house.

Those early days of widowhood must have nearly driven my mother to a nervous breakdown. We used to get very frightened when she threatened to put us all in the Workhouse and absolutely terrified when, in desperation she said, more than once, that she would "go and make a hole in the water." We knew what she meant and the river was not far away.... Later on when we had the luxury of a gas cooker she was always going to put her head in it, but when she was very, very angry with us and she had just about reached the end of her tether, she had apparently changed her mind about putting an end to herself ... and was going to put an end to us! Or that's what she implied, for she would scream furiously, "I'LL

SWING for you yet!" Young as we were we knew what that meant too.

But we stayed alive and as the years went by got used to hearing these outbursts and knew they were empty threats. It was just her way of letting off steam.

Chapter 6

She must have been glad to get us out from under her feet. What a strange expression that is, but in our crowded conditions, it truly summed it up. Children were accepted at school when they were four years old and in exceptional circumstances, when they were three, so at least we were out of the way for five days a week, and what a blessing.

I loved school and worshipped the teacher. In wintertime the school, perched high on top of Windmill Hill, was a haven of warmth and comfort. In the infants' room there was a magnificent coal fire and many times when I began to look a bit mauve I was allowed to sit in my little wooden chair right up close to it, revelling in the luxury.

There were hot pipes around the walls in the cloakroom and in the other classrooms. I used to sit on these during the playtimes while the other children ate their mid-morning snacks. There was a smell of soap, saffron cake, orange peel and apples about the cloakroom. I never felt the need to eat anything at school but sometimes, if someone's apple looked tempting I would ask for the core and suck away at it contentedly with the warmth od the pipes right against my bottom.

At Christmastime the Mayor of the town always visited the school and each child was presented with an orange and some sweets. The Headteacher too was very generous and we each received a hankie and a card. Even such a small square of material was a valued item in those days and many of us went around with our hankies pinned on our chests with large safety pins so that we would not lose them.

In the Infants' department, I learned to read and write quite quickly and was soon moved up to the next class. I was not particularly interested in making paper balls or modelling in clay or plasticine. I liked a lead pencil in my hand, or a slate on which I could scratch all manner of words and wipe them off again and again. I loved the smells of the classroom, the chalk, the pencil shavings, the flowers in the windowsills and the comforting, motherly smell of the teacher.

We did not learn by the play way although of course it was not all work. There were singing games like, 'Fair Rosie is a Lovely Maid' and 'The Farmer's in his Den', but mostly it was learning to read and write, and learning our tables so that we could do sums. How satisfying it all was, and with what love and dedication the two infants' teachers put us through our paces.

It was not hard work to do our word building or to learn our tables. As we did it every day, it all came naturally somehow, and most of us looked forward to getting up to Standard One where we would use ink and pens and begin to do 'double writing' instead of script.

By the time my father died I was beginning to show promise of being a good scholar. I took a delight in all that I did at school ad had a good retentive memory. I filled my exercise books with compositions which made my teacher laugh and I had a flair for number work which allowed me to work out simple problems, mostly about men and their work as I remember!

The teacher was a gem. She took us for needlework as well as all the other subjects and provided us with endless entertainment as we stitched away and she told us Brer Rabbit stories using a broad Cornish accent. She was a remarkable woman, wedded to her work but not a fully trained teacher. She just had a knack with children. Her name was Miss Dew, which in itself was an appropriate name but Miss Do would have been even more apt. She lived on the outskirts of the town and everyday walked the one-mile to the school, down one hill and up the other longer one. She always moved at great speed and had not a surplus ounce of fat on her bones. The pointed umbrella that she inevitably carried seemed to be propelling her up that final climb to the school that was her life.

What a strange assortment of children we were. The workhouse children stood out a mile, even amongst the poorest of us, and I was not the only one of them. The boys wore hob nailed boots and corduroy trousers. Nobody who was anybody wore corduroy in those days; it was a sign of extreme poverty. The girls wore boots too, and aprons, but they were certainly not meant to protect any finery. The workhouse children smelled of carbolic soap and some of them were not very bright. Who knew what brought them to the starkness of the workhouse or what they had suffered? But it made no difference. Most of them made good eventually and became very respected citizens.

We did not all wear hobnailed boots but our shoes had to last so we had protectors nailed on their soles. With such an assortment of metal on the heels and toes of our footwear it was a mercy that the floors were plain board and not highly polished as in so many schools of today.

In earlier years most of us had worn gaiters in the winter to keep our legs warm. They were fleecy lined and made of soft brown leather, reaching to above our knees. What an age it must have taken to put them on and take them off for they had a long row of buttons down each outside leg and it must have been a difficult task indeed for young fingers. At home we used a buttonhook but there was no such aid at school where we had to remove our gaiters.

Later on, Wellington boots began to appear in the shops. They were very expensive so only a few pairs appeared in the classroom on the feet of the more fortunate among us. That they were unhealthy for the feet if worn in the warmth of the classroom made no difference. They were high fashion and if I could have owned a pair I would have been in Seventh Heaven.

The next best thing to actually owning them was to be allowed to wear them occasionally as we sat at our desks. And so, on many occasions I found myself actually revelling in the luxury of the shiny, fleecy-lined, rubbery smelling novelties while my friend, showing great self-sacrifice, wore my shabby shoes. How I loved the flap of those boots against my legs as I walked out to the teacher's desk to have my work marked. And then, back at my desk again I would take an admiring look down at my encased legs and feet and sigh with sheer bliss. But no amount of pleading would allow me to wear those objects of delight outside the classroom. As far as I was concerned, they were for indoors only.

They must have been magic boots for there was no holding me as regards my schoolwork. If we had completed the work designed for Standard One we were moved up, irrespective of age, so soon I was rubbing shoulders with the children in the higher classes.

My next teacher was Mr. Blank but there were certainly no blanks in his teaching of the Three R's. He was not college trained either and therefor could never be a Headteacher, or such was the talk that went on among the grown ups. Everybody thought the world of him, parents and children alike and I continued to thrive on all he taught me.

Often he read aloud to us as we followed, surely an excellent way of learning both the skills of oral and written expression. We read too of course, around the class, and woe-betide anyone who had lost the place. It was rather tedious when the weaker brethren were struggling through their paragraphs, but as we had to keep our eyes glued to the page in case we were suddenly asked to continue, most of us took in the spelling and punctuation with no trouble and without realising we were doing so.

Our favourite book was 'Splendid Spur' and after play each day and back in the classroom we would all have our hands up chanting, "Splendid Spur please Sir! Splendid Spur, please Sir?" I am sure that I did not realise at the time what a splendid spur this teacher was to so many pupils.

And so it was, that when I was not yet ten-years old I found myself in the top classroom in Standard Six and being taught by the Head Teacher. There I was, in the top class almost, a skinny little soul, pale and bespectacled and with an obsession for school. But come to think of it, I was not all that good really. I could write nicely and spent hours practicing it both at home and at school. I could spell because I read such a lot, the same books over and over again, and I could do sums but I don't think I completely understood what I was doing. To my mind I was a flash in the pan and not nearly as bright as I was made out to be.

Chapter 7

After school I would run down Windmill Hill at such speed that I often fell over and grazed my knees. It was then that I limped with a tearful face to Auntie Min. She was the one to whom we always ran under such circumstances. Granny was too busy in the workroom and if my mother was home from work she would say impatiently,

"Oh wrap your hankie around it. It din going to kill you."

But Auntie Min would soothe with kind words and gentle hands. She knew what children needed even though she never had any of her own for she was always too busy looking after other people's and had never even considered marriage from what I could gather.

I loved her making a fuss of me. She would take a piece of kitchen paper as she called it and lick it before sticking it on my grazed knee. It was only a small piece of whiter paper but it worked miracles and took the place of the more elaborate plasters of today. The blood held it fast and there it stayed until the graze healed over and the by then very soiled piece of paper finally dropped off or was gently pulled away.

She must have pulled out more loose teeth than she could count. It was always done with a piece of cotton tied around the rocking tooth which somehow held on by its skin. She would talk to us soothingly all the time and then 'twick' it out before we realised what was happening. But if I had put any of my milk teeth under my pillow at night, I am sure that I would have found no sixpence there in the morning. The fairies were not around in my young days except in storybooks.

It's funny the number of times I had toothache. Now there was a fairy story if not a downright lie. I had only to hold my face and claim that it "hurt awful" and Auntie Min would get her precious bottle of whisky and the warming liquid would be lovingly massaged into my gums.

Occasionally, one or other of us paid a visit to the dentist because toothache was not always imaginary and a decayed tooth firmly entrenched in tender gums was not likely to respond to anyone's twicking. We did not have to make appointments. If I needed an extraction, I was taken to the dentist's house and ushered upstairs to the waiting leather chair and all its awesome attachments. The journey upstairs in vivid in my mind. Not that I was afraid - far from it. I knew I would feel no pain and I felt so important following this white-coated figure up the stairs that were thickly carpeted, a real sign of luxury in those days. The brasses glinting on the walls and the aroma of real coffee being percolated somewhere in the house added to the sense of occasion.

The dentist was always very kind and I loved the attention, especially when he shook hands with me as we left the house.

But it would not have done to go there too often for I knew very well that it cost a fortune to have one of my teeth removed - half a crown (twelve and a half pence) in fact, handed over as soon as the job was done.

You would think that I had had enough of pity but I was quite a little actress and loved attention. Some days when I came out of school, I put only one arm into the sleeves of my coat leaving the other sleeve dangle and my arm drawn up across the inside of my coat. Instead of running, I walked with a pained look on my face. It always had the desired effect and I delighted in the sympathy I saw on the faces of those grownups I met on my way home.

"Little monkey," my mother would say testily, "Why can't you wear your coat proper? Dragging on the buttons like that! I don't think you'm right in the 'ead."

But Auntie Min would see no fault in us. If we did anything silly it was always,
"Don't go on so. Tis child-like and they've got their funny little ways," when anybody reprimanded us. Like my grandmother she was an old lady all the time I knew her and she had no income except her Old Age Pension which was ten shillings a week. She was not our Auntie in the true sense of the word because she was a distant cousin of Granny's and had

become an orphan early in her life. She was born in Jersey too and when Granny went back there on her honeymoon, she brought Auntie Minnie back with her to give her a home.

She knew what she was doing for the two remained close until the end. You could not imagine one without the other in the same way that you could never imagine either of them being anywhere else but in that house in Westgate Street. There was a permanency about them. They seldom got ill and it seemed that they would live forever. Other people got ill and died, some of them when they were very young, but it never entered my head that either Granny of Auntie Min was running out of time on this earth.

On only one occasion did Minnie take herself off for a holiday. She went to London to stay with relatives and had hardly gone when Granny became mysteriously 'ill'. How could this be? She was as strong as an ox and was never known to have a headache. Yet here she was actually in bed and apparently about to breathe her last.

"You'll have to send for Minnie," she told her daughter. "She'll know what to do."

So Auntie Min came back and Granny recovered immediately. It couldn't have been God's will this time surely. It was more likely a fine piece of acting on her part, or it could have been that she simply could not exist without that other part of her being by her side, and that she was really ailing.

I often wonder why everybody called that other half of Granny, Auntie Min. Her real name was Louisa Le Breton. In my early days I had always thought this was Louisa the Briton, but anyway it was very dignified sounding name and certainly she lived up to it even in the very late years of her life.

She was upright in stature and character. Her face was practically unlined and I never saw a grey hair in her head. She had the sort of face that nuns have and there was the same sort of serenity about her whole being. Not that I can imagine nuns putting their hair in curling pins each night, but this was one piece of vanity that she did allow herself. However did she sleep with her hair wound so tightly round those little metal instruments of torture so close to her head? Indeed how did she see well enough in her candle lit room to put them in? As I wrote before, she slept in the attic, always referred to as 'the top of the house'. The window was no more than the size of a large shoebox and was opened only perhaps to shake out a duster. It's a wonder her head was not touching the ceiling and scraping it with her curling pins when she finally got into bed each night after saying her prayers. But she slept in that attic room for many, many years and until her ninetieth birthday kept in good health. Them when she eventually had to sit with her legs resting on a stool she would say,

"I don't understand it. I don't know what's gone wrong with my knees."

She was Granny's right hand and more besides, though she was often 'bossed around' by the head of the house. She could turn her hand to anything it seemed. She helped with the dressmaking, the cooking, the cleaning and the children - most of all, the children. Granny's seven had all been born without the aid of a doctor. Usually, a kindly neighbour was all the extra help required but on one occasion it was all over before even she got there. Minnie was always there to help. The one bore children and the other looked after them. They were like her own sons and daughters.

I do not think that it ever occurred to her that she was being put upon. What she did was done with love and devotion. The only payment she received was her 'keep', or at least that was what the arrangement was all the time that I knew her. It may have been different in her younger days as she had learned dressmaking in the workroom along with all the other apprentices and may have been able to earn a little money of her own when she became skilled.

Auntie Mabel was my father's youngest sister and as her husband was away for long spells in the Navy she lived with the two old ladies. We always considered that she lived a lady's life with Granny to help with the housekeeping and Auntie Min to do the harder work and look after the children. But she was a devoted daughter and cared for the old souls in the later years. It must have been a great trial towards the end but she never complained or lost patience with either of them. Even when, nearing one hundred years old, Granny finally became bedridden it would have been unthinkable to put her into any kind of institution.

When my Aunt's four children were born they too became Minnie's boys and then of course there were the three children in my family. Perhaps we did not mean quite so much to her for she had not actually helped bring them into this world, but we were Oldridge's children, and how she had loved him.

No wonder her face was so serene. I cannot think of any sin of which she could be accused. Perhaps she was rather too narrow minded, but that is hardly a sin. She was always telling us to be good and that God saw everything that we did. We must not tell lies or use bad words. Even the word 'fool' was loathsome to her. She used to quote,
"He who calleth his brother a fool is in danger of Hell Fire."

How she could bring herself to use the word I do not know, but as it was reckoned to be a quotation from The Bible I suppose it did not count as a swear word. How she must have cringed when my mother came out with things such as,

"Go to hell," or "You mind your own bloody business!" On Granny's side of the house we never heard this sort of talk but on our side it was commonplace. As my mother said,

"You've got to give way to your feelings sometimes." And who could blame her?

We knew the difference between right and wrong alright, and we knew what would happen to us if we did bad things. You had to be good if you wanted to go to Heaven and when you died, and if you were wicked, well you went to prison. And you would have to live on bread and water. That would have been dreadful and too awful to contemplate. However, could I exist without my soaked crust and Sunday cream? But worse than that, if you were really bad then you would go to hell - there was that word again, but apparently it was all excusable, in that context....

So, on the whole we were good children. Sometimes we cheated when playing Ludo or Snakes and Ladders but perhaps God did not notice! And I often told lies but nothing very serious. It was usually at school and fantasy more than anything else. Other children had marvellous toys that they sometimes brought to school, so I had them too, but only in my imagination. I told of the marvellous doll I had which could walk and talk and had a different set of clothes for each day. It had cost pounds and pounds. Well, you couldn't really call it lies, could you?

But for all her narrow mindedness, Auntie Min was always ready to make allowances. As well as her famous, "It's only child-like," she came out with,
"Leave them alone, do. Boys will be boys," or "You can't expect them to be perfect." And sometimes if any of us did or said something for which she could find no excuse she would simply say disapprovingly,
"What sense!" It was a catchphrase in the family for years after she'd gone.

And though we had thought she would live forever in that house alongside my grandmother, at the age of ninety-one, not long after that other splendid old lady who lived to her one hundred and first birthday. It appeared that one could not live without the other and we all knew that Minnie would not last long once they were finally parted.

I regret that I never actually told either of them what they meant to me and how much I felt I owed them. When one is young so much is taken for granted. If Auntie Min was beside me now, reading what I have written about her, I know what she would say. A look of pleasant surprise would come over her face and then, almost lost for words, she would purse her lips and say,

"What sense!" But I hope that it would not have been said disapprovingly.

Chapter 8

Of course we all attended Sunday school. On the one hand it was good for our souls and on the other it provided peace for the grownups on a Sunday afternoon and something for us to do.

As far as I was concerned it was a good idea to go to Sunday school for then in the summer I could go on the annual outing to the seaside. On the appointed day we all assembled in the town square after a service in the church of St Mary Magdalene.

"Never mind about praying," we thought, "Let's get to The Square quickly, and try to get a charabanc without those tiresome people who always get sick on the journey."

The charabancs were real boneshakers. There were not many cars on the roads in the 1920's and to be able to ride in any motor vehicle at all was a tremendous treat. The charabancs had their names artistically painted on the back of each one: one was 'Dunheved', another 'Valencia' and still another 'The Gem'. This last one did not live up to its name and had to be avoided at all costs.

It was a mad scramble, with children chattering excitedly, buckets and spades rattling and mothers dong their best to establish a little order. But at least we were all settled in and the luck ones found seats in the back that was supposed to be the most comfortable ride.

We rattled along the roads, cheering like mad if our vehicle managed to pass another and moaning inwardly if we had to stop because someone was being sick. Sometimes we did not have to stop because the seaside buckets were handy, and anyway the driver was as eager to get to the end of his journey as we were. All that chatter and singing.... It was enough to burst his eardrums. Who would be the first to get a glimpse of the sea? Hurrah! There it is, glinting in the sunshine. We could not get there fast enough.

And then what happened? No sooner had we got out and stretched our legs than our mothers announced that they wanted a cup of tea before proceeding to the beach. With what impatience we endured this annual ritual, "Come on. Come on! You're wasting precious time," we thought.

A day at the beach circa 1926 with Granny Body, Auntie Min (Louisa Le Breton), Auntie Carrie and Auntie Mabel

At last we got to the beach and started making our sand castles. Then it was a paddle in the sea. We had no bathing costumes, most of us, so it was a case of tucking our clothes into our knickers and taking to the water that way. They were memorable days, especially if the weather was kind. But, after all the excited anticipation, on some occasions the Sunday School Outing turned out to be a fiasco. The rain that the vicar had prayed for earlier in the summer was known to come down in buckets on the day and as one of the children was heard to say on such an occasion,

"Isn't God piggish?"

Then, as Christmas drew near we were all looking forward to our prizes for good attendance at Sunday school and presents on the Christmas tree. Our teachers marked a register just like at day school but we also had stamp books into which we stuck little Bible scene pictures for each attendance. If this book was filled with these stamps we could be sure of a good prize and a lovely present. The books were ones to treasure; we were encouraged to choose prayer books or Bibles but we never knew until the evening of the Christmas party what the tree would provide. What joy it all provided, and what happy memories of childhood the smell of a Christmas tree brings back.

I did not really need rewards to slock me to Sunday school or Church. I loved listening to the Bible stories and looking at the people in church. I was fascinated by the way some of them curtsied or bowed to the altar before moving into their seats, and the way they signed themselves with the cross. It all looked so very important. The old smell of the church mingled with the perfume of ladies of high fashion and sometimes the windowsills were filled with flowers or Harvest Festival offerings and then I reckon mine was the most thankful heart there.... But I didn't like the smell of the hyacinths that were used for Easter for they always made me think of funeral wreaths and not the joys of spring.

Sometimes I accompanied my mother to church for evening service, feeling very grown up. She did not go very often but nothing would keep her away if there was a special festival or her favourite visiting preacher was due. She never professed to being a Christian but she loved the hymns and reckoned more people would go to church regularly if there was more joyous singing and less "droning on of all they old prayers."

Often, when she came out of church she would say something like,
"Did you see Mrs So-and-so all dressed up to the nines? They'm all a lot of hypocrites. They only go to church to show off their fine clothes." I daresay she was right about some members of the congregation, especially those ladies who swept up the aisle to the front pews almost as if they were taking part in a fashion parade, and followed by their insignificant husbands.

But it all added up to the pleasure of churchgoing and we didn't have to hurry home afterwards because we were afraid of missing some long-running saga on the television. We did not even possess a wireless set. Instead we had an old wind-up gramophone with an enormous horn that my father had bought when we were better off than at this time. Songs, like 'Yes we have no Bananas', 'Don't have any more Mrs. More' and "It ain't goin' rain no more' were very popular but when we ran short of money a relative bought the gramophone from my mother and that was the end of that.

Sunday was a day of rest however, and even the playing of a gramophone would have been frowned upon. I can almost hear Auntie Min saying,
"What sense!" if the strains of such music had reached her ears on that Holy day.

On my grandmother's side of the house no work was done on Sundays except the preparation of meals. People could be desperately waiting for the completion of their garments but not a stitch was put into them on the day of rest. It was The Sabbath Day and since we knew the Ten Commandments off by heart it was clear that we were meant to keep it holy. Nor could we play games of any kind, either indoors or out. We could go to church or Sunday school or "Go for a nice walk" but except for reading there was not very much to do. And if Christmas Day fell on a Sunday it was agony waiting for the next day when we could play without feeling that we were breaking God's laws.

All this made such an impression on my young mind that I often had dreams about it. In one dream I discovered in Church doing my knitting that was a dreadful crime indeed. I don't know what happened to me as a result of this for I woke up in fear and relieved to discover that it had not really happened. To have done any knitting on a Sunday was unthinkable, but to actually be doing it in church! Well....

My mother could not put up with such humbug and found plenty to do. If she was working in other people's houses during the week she had to catch up with things at home when she could. And that was on Sundays.

"The better the day, the better the deed," she would say defiantly or, "Cleanliness is next to Godliness."

And so she kept her two rooms and her three children spotless: It was almost an obsession with her.

Chapter 9

On weekdays we could play to our heart's content, especially in the summer. Behind the house was a large, sloping open space that for some inexplicable reason we called the Sheep Market. All the children of the area congregated there to play their games and because there was little traffic we could also play safely in the street outside the house.

We did not need many toys for our play. If you had a bouncing ball, a piece of rope or five smooth stones you could enjoy yourself for hours at a time. We played hopscotch with our friends but even by yourself you could throw a ball against a wall and invent many ways of improving throwing and catching. A rubber ball was a prized possession and the one I had lasted for many years and was a beautiful bouncer even when bits had worn off it. How I loved its rubbery smell and the smoothness of its surface when I first had it.

We played five stones in small groups. What an achievement to be able to throw one stone into the air and pick up the other four before it came down again. Nowadays in schools it is thought necessary to go to great lengths to create similar skills in young children. Teachers talk about dexterity, motor control and co-ordination. They go out of their way to teach such things, but to us they came naturally; we were our own teachers in this respect.

It is the same with drama. "Children must be helped to act out their aggression and encouraged to use their imagination through free drama," we are told. But here again we provided our own drama experiences. We played Mothers and Fathers, Doctors and Nurses (inevitably), and Cowboys and Indians. We acted out all kinds of stories and needed no grownups to show us the way. It was a natural part of childhood and of growing up. We jumped and climbed and chased and were happy.

A great deal of sharing went on among the children in our household. There was a wooden hoop which we could take it in turns to bowl around the houses, and later an iron one which needed rather more skill to move along as it was attached to the hooked metal rod with which we propelled it. There were bits of wood we could use for bats and there was always my father's old workshop where we could get up concerts to entertain the grownups.

Winter had its compensations too and snow was always welcome. We had no sledges or toboggans, but a large tin tray was all we needed. With o traffic to worry about we could trudge to the top of Windmill Hill as far as the school gates and then whizz down to the bottom, lying flat on our tummies on the tray, our cheeks reddened by the excitement.

The boys also concocted 'geris' or go-carts out of orange boxes and the like. They were always on the lookout for old perambulator wheels and were proud of the vehicles they knocked together. There were exciting races up and down the street or down Sheep Market hill and even the girls liked to have a go at steering these marvellous speedsters. A few children had pedal motor cars bought at great expense and a bit of a show off, but they were not nearly so much fun as the home-made gerries.

The children on Granny's side of the house were rather more fortunate than the ones on our side. After all, their father was in the Navy so there was no real shortage of money there. They had a regular supply of comics that we could enjoy as well. I could revel in the antics of Weary Willie and Tiger Tim, and read 'Comic Cuts' over and over again. Tiger Tim appeared in a splendid comic and even famous Hollywood stars like Harold Lloyd and Buster Keaton appeared in some of the comic strips. Each day brought it own special comic for that week and I was always waiting for my cousins to finish with their copies so I could get at them. I read those comics, every word, over and over again until I almost knew them off by heart.

On Saturday afternoons we could go to the pictures, especially if something special was being screened like a Mary Pickford or a Jackie Coogan film. It was three pence to go in and sit on the forms in the very front of the cinema, but there was always Auntie Min and she would see to it that we went, along with all the other children. The cinema was known locally as 'The Flea Pit' and if a jungle film was being shown, people were heard to say that there were more animals in the seats than on the screen.

We sat so near to the front that it was a wonder we could see the screen at all, but with our heads tilted back and our necks aching with the strain we thrilled to the jungle adventures and laughed fit to burst our sides at the genius of Charlie Chaplin and the antics of Felix the Cat. The lady pianist must have had a crick in her neck too for she glued her eyes to the screen and played suitable music for each scene.

I loved the sad bits, especially those involving mothers and fathers and their children. It must have been about this time that we saw 'Uncle Tom's Cabin', 'East Lynne' and Little Lord Fauntleroy' and undoubtedly I had a good weep over those. We used to identify with the actors and actresses.
"That's me!" one of us would shout, followed by a chorus of, "No it din. That's me." I rather fancied myself as Pola Negri, and nobody wanted to be the villain it seemed.

And so we passed exciting Saturday afternoons, lost in wonder at the magic of the silver screen and grinding our sweets as we watched. There was a Dickensian sweet shop next to the cinema, the same shop from which I usually fetched the Sunday cream. When the advertisements came on we could go out and buy some sweets if we had a penny or two left over, but not all of us could afford the pictures and sweets in one afternoon. However, as Granny said, "God will provide," and sure enough he did, in the shape of the old man who was the usher at the cinema. I believe his name was Mr. Shear but to me he will always be remembered as Mr. Cheer for he was always smiling and knew who were the unfortunates among us. A penny for this one, a penny for the other and most of us had our sweets to chew. We were always warned never to take sweets from strangers but Mr. Cheer was certainly no stranger and no dirty old man. Even at that young age when playing in the Sheep Market or in the street it was easy to know whom it was best to avoid in this respect. You somehow knew who was nice and who was not.

It would seem that I was always 'on the scrounge' for pennies to buy this or that. But when you are very poor you know who will be softhearted and how to play up to them. Uncle Charlie from London had a good job as a printer for one of the well-known national newspapers and whenever he came on holiday with his family we could be sure of his generosity. We probably had more sweets then than was good for us and it was not unusual for him to give me a whole half-crown all to myself. Not all of it went on sweets for it was a fortune to me and I could even put some of it in a moneybox after buying other little things I fancied.

Uncle Joe, my father's eldest brother was also good to us at Christmas. A large box would arrive containing gifts for each member of the household. We could not wait for Granny to unpack it and distribute the presents. What pleasure it must have given her too, handing out those treasures from the Big City, as head of the family. This uncle was the only one who had a car at that time. When he and his family came to stay we thought he must be very rich indeed although the car was small with seats that nearly touched the ground. I used to hang around when he was preparing to take his family to the seaside and because I could swim he often squeezed me in too so I could help his children with their swimming.

I started going to the local swimming bath at an early age. That I had no proper swimming costume made no difference. It was surprising what Granny could concoct from an old pair of cotton bloomers. A little bib stitched across the top and a couple of straps and I was a real bathing belle. At first the older girls in the school who coaxed me into the water until I could walk about with it up to my chin took me. It was all very daring and I would not be satisfied until I could swim and could actually go out to the deep end.

The sessions I attended were strictly for ladies and girls only. Men and boys had theirs quite separately for it was not considered decent for males and females to share the swimming baths at the same time. Sometimes when we were waiting to go in and the men and boys were still inside in their swimming suits I could peep through the door and see the forbidden sights. But if the attendant saw me peering in at them he would shut the door and tell me to keep my eyes to myself.

As time went by I was able to sport a real bathing suit, complete with sleeves, and even a bathing cap, a crinkly rubber affair that sat on top of my head and served no real purpose. But, it was all very grand, and so beautifully equipped how could I fail to learn to swim? Not for us the more sophisticated swimming aids of today but just wooden planks which we leaned over, splashing like made with our legs and eventually gaining enough confidence for the planks to be taken away.

Eventually mixed bathing was allowed. The powers that be had obviously decided that as swimming attire improved we were not all in danger of dying with laughter at such sights, though the state of the water was such that we were I danger regarding our health. The bath was not very big and the water was not changed very often. The level must have been raised quite considerably by the calls of nature that occurred when people were in the water and could not be bothered to get out!

It was amazing how many activities I fitted in as a child. I was a Brownie and a member of the Band of Hope, and for full measure, joined the Busy Bees where we seemed to spend most of our time knitting kettle holders for our mothers. And yes, I was also a Young Briton, which was a Conservative organization. My grandmother and her family were staunch Tories and when there was an election everybody, including the children, went about wearing their rosettes or coloured ribbons to show which side they were on.

The Conservative candidate was Squire Williams who lived on his estate only a few miles from our town. The Liberal candidate was Croyden Marks and although as children we had little idea as to what it was all about, we used to sing:

> Vote, vote, vote for Mr. Williams,
> Throw old Marksy in the sea.
> If I had a lump of lead
> I would throw it at his head
> And he'd never come to Launceston any more.

What a disappointment I must have been to the old folks when, many years later, I announced that I was going to vote Labour. Whatever next? I'm sure Auntie Min must have said, yet again, "What sense!"

What sense indeed....

Chapter 10

Fortunately for my mother the school holidays were not long ones. But as soon as we broke up she could get rid of me anyway for I was bundled off to stay with my mother's people who lived in a tiny village about five miles away. My aunt had no little girl of her own so from my very earliest days I was a welcome guest in her small cottage which she and her husband shared with her mother. I continued to spend my holidays with this aunt well into my teens for she had clearly chosen me to be her substitute daughter.

The granny here did not enjoy good health like the one at home. She was a crippled by arthritis and although she too was an excellent needlewoman she could not now use her fingers and was unable to do very much for herself. She eventually became bedridden for many weary years.

She had endured a hard life being the mother of eight children and with very little money coming in, even when her husband was alive. She lived by the Bible and in her later years when she could barely turn the pages with her swollen fingers, she managed to read a passage from The Good Book as she called it, each day. She even used biblical phraseology in her own speech and came out with expressions like,
"Hath her now?" and 'Doth her?"

She had numerous grandchildren her eldest daughter having herself produced thirteen of them. Goodness knows how she found names for all those regular little visitors, or how she remembered who each one was, but she too was a remarkable mother and as each of her children grew up and got married was a regular visitor at the local auction sales and helped get them set up ion their various houses. It was her proud boast that she had not lost one of her brood.

Granny had not reared all her children however. One of her daughters fell victim to diabetes when she was very young and I was told about how she had tried to cure her. A gypsy at the door had said that if she could be persuaded to eat a mouse she would recover from her illness. The family was desperate to try anything as the girl was dying before their eyes and they were desperate. So a mouse was caught, killed and prepared for cooking in the same way a chicken would be. Then the flesh was finely chopped and fed to the unfortunate girl. She did not know what she was eating of course as it was disguised amongst her other food, but it was of no use and she eventually died.

"Oh well," everybody said, "She was too good to live. A little angel if ever there was one." I loved hearing the stories these country folk told, all with a sense of the dramatic, and as the holidays approached I always looked forward to hearing other such tales, both sad and comic.

As soon as we broke up from school, out came a battered little tin trunk which did not fasten properly, and off I went for the customary visit to the country, at first by pony and trap and later on a canvas topped van. It was only a few miles away but it was like going to another world where everything was different from home.

My uncle worked on a farm and lived in a tied cottage, the middle one of three. The front door opened directly into the small living room that boasted as well as the usual table and chairs, a kitchen dresser. a prickly black sofa and, best of all, a pedal organ. Everything was spick and span and cosy. The large clock ticking away o the wall added to the warmth and feeling of friendliness in this room.

My aunt took great pride in the blue grey stone slabs that made the floor, covered here and there with bits of coconut matting. It was a good thing that the floors were not carpeted for in the winter muddy water sometimes came flooding into the cottage from the sodden churchyard on the higher ground behind the buildings. And then what a commotion there was, mopping and restoring the place to peace and order once more. It was all very worrying for my aunt seeing her furniture so threatened, but I loved being there when it happened. It was something out of the ordinary that appealed to my sense of drama.

All the cooking was done on the black stove which almost filled one wall and produced such mouth-watering items as saffron cake, Cornish pasties, biscuits and splits in abundance. My aunt was an excellent cook and it seemed that she could do anything which was to do with home-making, the result no doubt of being in domestic service for the years before her marriage.

How anyone could be such a competent cook in those conditions remains a mystery to me. There was no electric, no gas and not even a tap for the cold water supply. There was not even a sink in which to prepare her vegetables and therefore nowhere convenient to strain them once they were cooked. Yet at mealtimes the table was covered with a dazzling white cloth and the food was always perfect.

All the same, that we did not fall victim to some dreadful disease was a miracle. The lavatory was in the garden up the road and quite a distance if you were dying to go. And what did you find when you got there? A little box-like shed perched by the roadside hedge containing a wooden construction with a hole in the top concealing a bucket. At least we could pull the plug at home even if the lavatory was out in the yard. The contents of the bucket were periodically emptied into the garden and, I trust buried, but apparently it did not harm and probably accounted for the wonderful crop of rhubarb and the dahlias which were the best in the village.

Water was fetched from a pump still farther away up the road and in the middle of the village. It was carried in pitchers and buckets and for tea making was boiled in a huge back kettle that lived on top of the living room range. What intricate things were those black stoves of long ago. They served as room warmers as well as cookers and were operated either open or closed. When open the fire crackled merrily and by the removal of various covers the flames were directed upwards instead of across, over the top of the oven. Sometimes the fire needed coaxing to make it burn satisfactorily and a large pair of bellows, kept hanging on the wall nearby, were used to puff the reluctant flames in to action. My aunt did all manner of boiling on the fire. She also fried bacon, eggs and mashed potato in a large black iron pan as the sticks spluttered and spat, the sap almost oozing into the food. But there was never any problem with food sticking to the pan!

Frequently what looked like long, black instruments of torture were used, the tools for replacing rings and putting the stove to 'draw'. What a performance! But with coal added to the sticks the flames were soon leaping across the enclosed top of the oven and getting it hot enough to receive the baking of the day.

Cleaning the stove was the ritual of the week. It was very much like polishing shoes but done with black lead instead of shoe polish. The end product of all this rubbing and polishing was a joy to the house-proud working class women of that time. They were not satisfied until they could almost see their faces in the satin black gleaming surfaces.

And with so many smuts flying about and black smoke often billowing over everything, how could anyone produce such immaculate laundry work? But having washed it and carried it to the clothes line in the garden and several yards up the road, it was satisfying to have it all dried, damped and rolled down ready for the box iron which would put the finishing touches to it all.

The box iron was the shape of an electric or gas iron of today, but deeper. It had a space inside into which identically shaped pieces of iron could be placed with tongs when red hot, and which, used alternately, kept the iron at the required temperature. The mind boggles at such a complicated procedure that and the fact that the articles to be ironed did not end up dirtier than they were before they entered the washtub!

A prized possession was an Aladdin Lamp that also needed much care and attention to wicks and funnels if it was to work efficiently. This was only used to light the room downstairs and again it was a candle that normally served to light us to bed. The lamp and the shadows it made in the room fascinated me. Sometimes it would 'smitch' and produce long, black cobwebby ropes around the walls and pictures.
"The dratted thing," my aunt would say and hastily put a duster on a sweeping brush to get rid of the offending smuts.

To me it really was an Aladdin's Lamp. I would watch the many different moths as they circled around the shad, bumping almost against it and feeling the warmth of the light which attracted them, and I would listen to the crickets chirping in the hearth and feel the plush table cloth which was used between meal times and it was like being in a magic cave. Even better than all this were the sessions around the organ. Auntie Ethel played and I sang, mostly hymns. My shrill little voice must surely have thrilled any listeners as I struggled through 'Jesus Wants Me for a Sunbeam' and 'Jesus Bids us Shine.'

They were not all religious renderings, however, and I really used to let myself go with 'Uncle Tom Cobbley' and 'Old MacDonald had a Farm'. In fact I was considered good enough to take part in Pleasant Sunday Afternoon performance in the Chapel and if I had not been performing in God's house I'm sure I would have 'brought the house down' as the village people were delighted with such simple pleasures.

My aunt took great pride in me as well as the things in her cottage. Out would come the goffering iron with which she crimped the frills of her starched pillowcases and she would heat the tongs to put curls into my normally straight hair. Sometimes she singed bits off by mistake but no matter, when I appeared in front of the congregation I must have been a sight to behold. Sometimes she used another method to produce the desired effect and I often went to bed with my hair all rolled up in rags like Topsy. The next day when it seemed that my head did not belong to me the rags were removed and my hair coaxed into ringlets that, according to everybody, made me look like a little doll. With a huge bow of ribbon perched high on the top of my head I felt more like a tousled cat with its ears sticking up.

For a change I would be asked to recite instead of singing and although I expect my performance left a great deal to be desired they helped fill up the programme and pleased my aunt. She used to take part as well for she had a beautiful singing voice and her renditions included, 'Songs my mother used to sing' and I Know That My Redeemer Liveth'. What pleasant Sunday afternoons indeed with all the villagers dressed in their best clothes, squeaky shoes, camphor balls and all....

****

In the summer the highlights of my holiday were the visits to the cornfield where the men were harvesting. The corn was cut by horse-drawn machines and the sheaves were then made into tent shaped stooks and left to dry. In the afternoon we carried the men's 'drinking' to them so that they could work overtime and get the work finished before the weather changed. Tea drunk from enamel jugs, pasties and saffron cake went down as everyone sat on the prickly stubble while the steaming horses stood by waiting patiently to begin once more the monotonous journey around the still uncut stretch of corn. Then a swig of the farmer's cider helped the men to continue with their labours while the light lasted.

The women stood around in their starched print aprons, proud of the wholesome food they had brought for their men, while the children also had a 'bite to eat' before running off eventually to play hide and seek among the stooks or to gather blackberries from the hedgerows.

By the time the field of corn had shrunk to a patch of yellow no bigger than a very large tablecloth we were waiting breathlessly for the rabbits to run out of their last hiding place. The arrival of the machine had driven the terrified little creatures farther and farther towards the centre of the field as it wound threateningly round and round the perimeter of their haven, and now at last they would have to break cover.

They would run and so would we and throw ourselves upon the quivering masses of fur as they came out into the bewildering open field, too dazed to know in which direction to run. There was always someone nearby to take our catches off us and swiftly break the necks of those gentle animals.

I loved it all yet hated it. One minute a rabbit was a pulsating living creature and the next it was dead, tossed to join all the others in a heap by the hedge with flies buzzing around their glazed eyes. But it was no good being squeamish; rabbits were a menace but could be put to good use. Other animals met the same fate as the rabbit and it was all part of everyday life.

My uncle, as well as the neighbours, kept pigs in the yard behind their cottages and chickens too had the free range in their large wire-netted run in the garden. I watched the pigs in their sties as my aunt fed hem with their own special meal supplemented by kitchen scraps, and I knew the day would come when their squeals would rent the air as the knife struck into their necks. Then, as now, there was great activity; very dead, they were scalded and cut up ready for storage.

I could never bear to watch this dreadful slaughter but often saw the poultry being killed. To the men and boys of the village it was a simple procedure - pick out the bird which looks the plumpest, slit its throat with a penknife and then hang it up by the legs until it is still. It all seemed so brutal but I was assured that the poor bird hanging there upside-down and still struggling was dead alright, and that it was its nerves which made it twitch like that.

What meals the poultry provided - plenty for us and for the many cats that kept down the rats and mice that lurked in the yard and scampered among the faggots of wood stacked outside the back doors. The cats had to be kept down too, so usually when the kittens were born they were either promptly drowned or, because it was less trouble, hurled against the pigsty door even before they had a chance to breathe.

I do not suppose that it occurred to anyone that I might be upset by all this violence. After all, they had all been brought up with it as a natural course of events and it would have been surprising if they had shown any signs of sensitivity.

My cousins, both boys, who lived in the cottage next door, were older than I and had had to sort for themselves at an early age as their mother was a semi invalid. They probably had little patience with a mere girl who just hung around wide eyed at everything that was going on.

Sometimes I would go to their cottage and sit on a stool in the chimney corner. There was no range there but instead of a fireplace big enough to accommodate a whole faggot of wood at a time if required. The clone oven was a hole, high up in the wall and the kettles and cooking pans hung from chimney crooks which hung over the flames. It was fascinating to watch the baking being hooked off the primitive oven, and then to join the men folk as they sat on a wooden form to partake of their meal from a stark, scrubbed wooden table.

In the other cottage lived the village carpenter who had a daughter about the same age as me. We liked to play houses and the carpenter's shop was a handy place to collect ingredients from for cooking. Sawdust was a fine substitute for flour and mixed with water made excellent make-believe cakes and buns. They were much better than the ordinary mud pies.

There was always a place in the hedge or a tree which could serve as our house, and when we had found one we set about finding suitable crockery for or own little place. Sometimes we were lucky enough to have discarded cups and saucers to enact our imaginary housekeeping, but most often we collected shards from rubbish tips and arranged these broken pieces of crockery on the branches that made excellent shelves.

It was odd that this kind of play appealed to me for I did not take kindly to helping in a real house and my mother often referred to me as a lazy little monkey. It was all very tedious when I was expected to help my aunt and there were real dishes to dry, real dusting to do and real beds to make. She believed in 'bringing me up proper' and even a small girl must make herself useful.

I was much happier with my head in a book or visiting places of interest in the village. I liked to go and see the men working in the tailor's shop. It was so clever the way they chalked around the patterns and then cut out the cloth with giant scissors. I had seen Granny doing the same sort of thing but it was more interesting to see grown men sewing and sitting cross-legged as well, almost like gnomes on toadstools. The population of the village was small and I wonder where the tailor got his customers for the men folk around could not afford new suits very often and they were worn only once a week when they attended church or chapel.

I also liked to visit the blacksmith's shop set in the centre of the village near the communal pump. Since there were more horses around than cars when I was a small child there was always plenty of work for the smithy. It seemed like a place of torture tome with all those hot iron shoes being placed so firmly onto the feet of the horses and then hammered in with nails. I almost expected the poor animals to rear up in pain but they stood patiently throughout the procedure and did not flinch so I could rest assured that it was all quite painless.

The men who worked on the farms and those whose job it was to care for those splendid animals the cart horses, tending them in all kinds of weather, were proud of their charges and they were always turned out to perfection. Uncle Tom next door was one of these. His ruddy, weather-beaten face bore witness to the time he had spent behind the horses ploughing, reaping driving the haulage carts and taking well-groomed horses to the local horse show held each year.

For him it was work, work and more work and I do not suppose he had a holiday in the whole of his life. Even on Sundays, whatever was said about keeping the Sabbath Day holy, he had to set off early in the morning to see to the horses and help with the other animals. He wore an old jacket and cloth cap, corduroy trousers tied below the knee with binder twine, leather leggings and hobnailed boots. And if it was wet, an old sack around his shoulders completed his outfit.

There was not much leisure time and the wages were very poor indeed. Probably the highlight of Uncle Tom's life was the time he received a certificate for long service on the same farm presented to him at the Horse Show. And when he died his coffin was lowered into the mud and slush he had been accustomed to all his life, and the injustice of it all was not lost upon those at the funeral.

"Poor old Tom," they said, "What a life. What a bloody life!"

Oh yes, it was all very well for me. I only spent holidays in that village and through the years, the hardships experienced by those who toiled never entered my head. A man could give a lifetime of loyal service to his master and then find that when he could no longer work he had no roof over his head because he lived in a tied cottage and a new workman wanted to move in.

And when the summer was over and people were enjoying the season of mellow fruitfulness they went to their places of workshop and sang about ploughing the fields and scattering the good seed on the ground. They thanked the Lord with 'humble and thankful hearts' but I guarantee that many of those who sang with such fervour never gave a thought to the men responsible for such a bountiful harvest, those honest to goodness souls who were so often referred to as "only farm labourers"....

Chapter 11

Although I always enjoyed my holidays in the country I was always glad to get back to school but at one time when I was very young I really disgraced myself. I announced to the infants' teacher that I knew a very nice piece of poetry. She stood me in front of the class expecting to hear a suitable rendering such as 'The Sands of Dee' that I had recited at the chapel. She was horrified when I came out with a very dirty little rhyme that my country cousins had delighted in teaching me. Clearly nothing like it had been heard in the classroom before, especially with the apparent approval of the teacher who had told the children to listen carefully. What a stir I caused. I was sent back to my seat and told never to use those words again. I was obviously a very naughty little girl and the teacher was going to speak to my parents about my behaviour.

She could not have been all that cross with me though for she didn't smack my legs as she did on several other occasions when I was not behaving properly. Little girls are notoriously spiteful and I could scratch and pinch as well as anybody else. But such things could not be allowed in the classroom and the teacher had to deal with it. Often I was put to stand on a chair so that she could more easily reach my spindly little legs. I never blamed her for putting me in my place in this way for it was all part and parcel of going to school and she looked so funny with her hair bobbing up and down as she smacked. But tears were often not far away and I used to press my tongue against my cheek and hang my head, suitably ashamed by my misdemeanors.

By the time I reached the top class however, I had left all this childish behaviour behind me and was apparently a model pupil. A new Head Teacher had been appointed and what a lot I owed him for there is no doubt he really pushed me along with my schoolwork. In those days the number of children who gained scholarships that would take them to grammar school judged a school. We had not heard of the 'Eleven Plus' but we knew all about the scholarship examination and clearly Mr. Pearson, being a new broom, was out to prove himself.

The examination was very much like the Eleven Plus except that as well as papers on arithmetic and written composition, we had to answer questions on a set book. In previous years the books had been 'Ivanhoe' which was considered difficult, and 'Westward Ho!' an equally hard book for youngsters to get through, but the year I was due to sit for the scholarship the set book was 'Splendid Spur'. I had enjoyed it so much that I'd read it several times and I could not believe my good fortune.

Usually from two to four pupils went for scholarships from schools the size of ours. Those who were not considered good enough for a higher education at the County's expense either stayed on at the elementary schools until they were fourteen, or if their parents could afford it, went as fee-paying pupils to either the boys' or the girls' grammar school or to other private schools. There was compensation for those who just missed scholarship; they could go to the grammar school but would have to pay for all their own books. Fee-paying pupils also had to pass and examination but I never heard of any child falling off this stepping-stone to a better education.

As I was only ten years old, I don't suppose I really understood what a grammar school education was all about, but I had heard people say that it was the means of getting a good job eventually and in previous years, pupils who had got scholarships were carried around on the shoulders of the other children and everyone made a great fuss of them so it seemed that it was something worth having. Even so, nobody mentioned the subject at home; perhaps they did not know much about it. My mother had so much to do and had no time to show any interest in my schoolwork, and even Granny and Auntie Min seemed quite outside anything that happened in the classroom.

Other children told of presents they would receive if they got a scholarship. Bicycles and scooters were the most usual carrots which were dangled in front of them, and those who thought that they hadn't a chance anyway declared that they weren't bothered because they didn't want to go to school until they were sixteen, so there!

I continued with my schoolwork as usual. I enjoyed it so much that at no time did I regard it in any way as preparation for the big examination. That was something you had to do as a matter of course and I had no thoughts of either success for failure, but clearly the Head Teacher had his own ideas and encouraged me in every way, I think he must have felt sorry for me, such a poor little thing, and fatherless. I had been quite pretty as a small child; fair haired and blue eyed but doll-like toddlers have a habit of becoming Plain Jane's later on.

I was small for my age with a sallow complexion and short mousey hair that seemed to hang around my head like seaweed. A pair of nickel-framed spectacles perched on my snub nose only worsened my general appearance. At one time I had thought it would be rather grand to wear glasses and had pretended that I could not see very well. It was just another way of drawing attention to myself and being important but I had no bargained for those ghastly things with which I was landed and which were free. As my mother laughingly remarked, I looked like an owl looking out of an ivy bush and eventually I refused to ever wear them again.

****

The day of the examination drew nearer. We had taken another test earlier that was always referred to as 'The Prelim'. I had no idea at the time what this actually meant but it sounded as if it were of great importance. It was really just a process of elimination so that only the better pupils would have to face the ordeal of the more difficult testing.

As pupils from several schools in the area were involved the examination took place in the grammar school itself, a stern test indeed, for how could anyone produce their best work in such unfamiliar surroundings? The school had once been a private residence and stood in its own beautiful grounds. It seemed strange to enter that building and have to go upstairs fort the test. It was all very awesome because everything about that school was different to what we had been accustomed.

I do not remember the detail of the actual examination but recall quite clearly the obstinate hair on my pen nib that seemed to make spidery trails all over my work. But then, I had no good luck token in my pocket whilst some of the other girls had various items on view that were meant to encourage Lady Luck to smile upon them. One girl had a piece of coal, another a horse shoe and yet another, a rabbit's foot. "Oh well," I thought dismally, "I don't believe in such things anyway." But it would have been nice if somebody at home had just wished me luck.

We used dip-in pens at that time, with wooden handles and metal holders into which we pushed the pen nibs after licking them to make them write better. I always had an inky middle finger, especially near the top where the pen rested, and on this day it seemed more mucky than usual and it was difficult to keep my page clean. On top of this, the grocery bill was awful and I couldn't get the farthings to come right.

The only consolation was 'The Splendid Spur" for I could answer all the questions and even produced a long paragraph on why I thought the author had chosen that title. Afterwards we all compared notes, mostly regarding the arithmetic paper and that horrible bill. If you got the same answer as everyone else you were over the moon but if not, well ... you must have slipped up somewhere.

Nobody thought much about it once the day was over; it was as if it had never happened. We had gone through the motions and the results would not be out for ages so now we could forget all about it and return to ordinary, everyday affairs. I had not been asked at home how I got on and I never thought it necessary to discuss it. Apparently, it was not important after all. Not until the results came out, anyway... and then I really was the centre of discussion.

****

I was playing ball outside the Drill Hall in Westgate Street where a large poster on the door invited young men to 'Join the Army and See the World'. It is strange how such things remain in one's mind. Suddenly I saw my brother running up the street towards me,

"I've got something to tell you," he said importantly. "Mr. Pearson has been to see Mum, and you've passed the scholarship ... you, and somebody else. Mum's not home from work yet so Granny wants you."

Obviously he had little idea of what it all meant. For all he knew I might be going off somewhere on a ship for good scholars. He was only eight and nobody had discussed it at home, but the fast that the Head Teacher had actually visited our home made it seem something worth passing on as quickly as possible.

I cannot remember what happened immediately after the news was given to me and I ran home with my brother, but the effect it had upon the people who lived around us as it generally became known was bewildering. The general opinion seemed to be that I would never attend the grammar school,
"Her mother can't afford it," they said.
"It wouldn't be fair on her brother and sister."
"She can't stay on at school until she's sixteen."
"If it was her brother it would be different, but education's wasted on a girl. They only go and get married." And so on....

Clearly my mother was not overjoyed at the prospect of her daughter going to another school. She didn't hold with "all that education". With all the discussions that were going on it was almost as if I'd committed a crime. Only Auntie Min voiced an opinion likely to make me think that I'd done anything worthy of praise, "Your father would have been so proud of you," she said quietly.

Granny did not have much to say about it either but events proved that she had decided she would do all she could to see me through the next phase of my life. My mother also gradually came round to the idea that there might be something in education after all, and since the neighbours had been so quick in trying to make her mind up for her, well, she would see about that! Let them mind their own bloody business and she would work out her own affairs. Nobody was going to tell her what to do!

And so it was decided, in spite of all the murmurings that I should become a pupil at the Horwell Grammar School for Girls.
"You won't like it," said some of my friends, "They're all stuck up at that school and don't speak to the likes of us." I did not take much notice of this because some of my friends were already at the school and they had not complained and were still certainly speaking to me. Anyway, I would never be stuck up. How could I be when we were so poor?

I never felt good enough. That was the trouble. I always regarded myself as just a little nobody....

Chapter 12

So began preparation for the great day when I would first set foot as a pupil in the new school. My mother went to see the Chairman of the Governors well known for his interest in the less fortunate children, and he managed to arrange a clothing grant for me, the sum of eight pounds a year to be paid in three, termly installments. The figure of two pounds, thirteen and four remains in my memory to this day and the amount stayed the same for the whole of the time I was at the school.

Unfortunately, the grants were not paid until nearly the end of each term so that it was not easy to get all the school uniform which was compulsory, but with the aid of kindly relatives I was eventually attired and equipped, ready for I knew not what.

An older girl from the school was going to call for me on the first day and I waited anxiously for the first sign of her. I was feeling very grand in my new outfit, but very strange too and no wonder. I must have looked as if I was still in mourning for my father for the school colours were black and white. Under my home-made overcoat I wore a pleated serge tunic which for economy's sake was miles too large, and this was held in, somewhere around my bony hips, by a braid belt with fringed ends and tied in a sailor's knot. I wore this over a starched white blouse with striped black and white tie and my underclothes consisted of combinations, a liberty bodice and thick woollen bloomers. My legs were encased in unaccustomed long black woollen stockings held up by black elastic garters which felt uncomfortably tight, and my new black patent shoes were so shiny I was almost afraid to walk in them in case I scratched the toecaps.

And the hat! It was of regulation style and obtainable in the local shops but Granny had made mine and it was undoubtedly the most incongruous part of the uniform. It was simply a black serge paper bag shaped affair that sat on my head like a square tea cosy. The corners were turned down at the sides and held in place by round black buttons the size of marbles. The school badge was sewn on the front, presumably to show that this incredible headgear really was a hat. The one I would be wearing in the summer was much more presentable, a white, wide-brimmed Panama hat with a band of black and white around it to show the school colours. It was kept firmly on my head with a piece of narrow elastic which went under my chin and I was so proud of that hat that if it rained I carried it carefully under my coat so that it would not go limp.

Uncle Charlie's contribution to my equipment was a real leather attaché case and he had even paid extra to have my initials printed on the side. What a beautiful smell it had, and so shiny. It seemed too good to use but it was to serve me well in the years to come.

In my other hand I carried a black shoe bag drawn in at the top with black tape and concealing my black plimsolls that had to be worn inside the school because of all the stairs. It would never do to have all those girls clattering up and down the stairs in their outdoor shoes. Granny had made the bag and embroidered my name on it so that I would not lose it.

At last my companion arrived and I set off towards the school walking stiffly at her side. My stockings were making my legs itch and my heart was thumping uncomfortably against my ribs. I need not have worried for there were other new arrivals besides myself, all feeling very nervous and the day passed fairly smoothly except for just one little setback.

There I was in that place of high learning and I had not brought any writing equipment with me! All I had inside my brand new case was a set of geometrical instruments, considered 'a must' if you were to benefit from a grammar school education, but these were not necessary on the first day or even during the next few weeks. Pens and pencils had been provided in the previous school and these small items had been overlooked in the endeavour to send me off clad the same as everybody else.

I nearly wept. It seemed so stupid to have forgotten the necessary tools for the job, but another girl, a farmer's daughter, had spares and thanks to her I was able to copy my timetable and settle down eventually to the day's work.

****

It was a small school and small must be beautiful. There were never more than a hundred girls on the register to an average of seven teachers, including the Head Mistress. Married women teachers were not employed until very many years later and there was little change in the staff during the whole of my time at the school. There was a permanency about it all for the teachers on the whole were wedded to their work and knew their pupils inside out. In other words they saw you through and through you! And it all added up to stability and the necessary continuity of work.

There was a great deal of regimentation in the school. Each day we went first to our classrooms and on the bell proceeded to the Assembly Hall for registration, accompanied by our form teachers. Prefects were strategically placed along the route to the hall to ensure that there was no talking or running, and we stood in our appropriate lines clutching the hymn books we each had to buy.

The Head Mistress appearing to take her place on the small raised platform in the front was an unforgettable sight. With her head tilted back and her academic gown billowing behind her she resembled a ship in full sail. At the end of each assembly, a chord was played on the piano as a signal to turn right and we marched out, a line at a time, to suitable military music. I almost felt I ought to salute as I passed the dias but woe betide anyone who put a hand or foot out of place or looked the least bit untidy.

The Headmistress had presence. Nobody could have mistaken her for an assistant teacher. She reigned supreme and could strike terror into the hearts of pupils and staff alike. It must have been her eyes for they seemed to penetrate into everyone's soul. She was slender in build and of undeterminable age. That is to say she was not young, and yet she never appeared to get any older. She had boundless energy and had no room in her school for slackness. To be called to her study seldom meant anything but trouble and standing on the rug in front of her desk we soon came to understand the true meaning of the phrase, 'on the carpet'.

There were plenty of rules and regulations and discipline was very strict, but for all that it was a very pleasant, well-run school and though at times some of the teachers were known as dragons, battle- axes or even worse, they had hearts of gold. The Headmistress frightened us to death at times but she had our welfare at heart and certainly had a soft spot for the unfortunates of the world. No tramp who ever came to the door of that school was turned away empty-handed and her own house was a refuge for the many stray animals that found their way to her door. She was reputed to have numerous cats under her roof but dogs had a special place in her heart. She was seldom seen without a dog, first one then another and for many years Pat, a black and white mongrel, usually lay at her feet throughout her lessons.

Her name was Lucy Constance Tindal-Atkinson, known to the less respectful as Tiddles but to everyone else as T.A. If we were doing anything wrong such as playing Consequences or Hangman when left on our own, the frantic warning, "T.A.'s coming!" was enough to send us scuttling to our desks and establish an atmosphere of complete silence. She didn't have to speak to us - one look from her was enough to make us quake and wish ourselves further.

We knew how far we could go with most of the staff. They were good teachers who stood no nonsense and we respected them. They were 'stayers' in every sense of the word and one did not easily forget the punishments they meted out. At one time a girl had thoughtlessly thrown some orange peel into the empty grate of the school hall. She never owned up so everybody in the school suffered because nobody was prepared to give her away. The result was that every girl in the school had to write out, one hundred times, 'No pleasure is comparable to standing on the vantage ground of truth.'

Obviously litter was something that would not be tolerated.

****

The first year went by very quickly and I found most of the work well within my scope. My best friend lived in the same street and me, but her father owned a fish and chip shop and he was able to pay for her education. By my reckoning he was very rich indeed especially since he was able to employ my mother for some days during the week. He was a generous man and often provided us with free fish and chips. In those days you could go to the shop and ask for "Two of each", a piece of crisply battered fish and two pennyworth of chips, or if you were really flush, "three of each" and that was a feast.

Once a week our class went to the boys' school at the other end of the town. We had no laboratory in the school and in order to chemistry it was necessary to take ourselves elsewhere. This weekly visit was something entirely new tome and it was clear from the start that I was never destined to shine at science.

The laboratory smelled of gas and other odd odours and as far as I was concerned was just a place where you did experiments that you didn't really understand, and then wrote notes about them in your best handwriting.

We manipulated Bunsen burners, made copper sulphate crystals, turned litmus paper blue and made several cylinders of oxygen but just went through the motions without taking much real interest. I produced beautiful drawings and never got less than nine out of ten for my written experiments, but it was obvious as the years went by that my visits to the boys' school were a waste of time. There was however, compensation to be found in the fact that as we went up the stairs to the lab we could sometimes get a glimpse of the boys through the open door of the classroom, and a smile from one of them was enough to make any girl's heart flutter.

Once a week too, I found myself back in my old school in order to do cookery and needlework and how I hated this. I could not afford the ingredients for cooking for one thing, and my material for sewing was often scrounged rather than bought. The teacher was a funny wizened little woman who for some reason was known as Murrumbidgee. Away from our normal school and the iron control of the Headmistress it seemed we could play up a bit and do what we liked, consequently I for one did not learn much from these sessions over the mixing bowls, and the teacher herself must have dreaded our every appearance in her domain, as base for other visiting schools as well as our own.

Children are often very cruel and we often made that poor little soul's life a misery. It was only after she retired and we were grown up that some of us, regretting our behaviour of long ago, felt compassion for her and sometimes visited her in her small cottage where she lived alone.

We had one hockey pitch, one tennis court and no gymnasium. We did 'drill' in the assembly hall in our ordinary clothes and many years later when it was suggested that the girls she do P.T. with their tunics removed, and wearing only their knickers and blouses, many of the girls and their parents were horrified. What if the caretaker should be passing the window? It would not be right for him to see young girls jumping about and showing their knickers in this way!

For the whole of the tie I was in that school it was not permitted for the girls to mix freely with the boys. Further up the road from us was another boys' school that was for fee-paying pupils only, both dayboys and boarders. That latter could be seen going to either church or chapel wearing their mortarboards and looking very elite indeed. On certain days they were allowed into town to do their personal shopping.

By the time we were fourteen we were either 'going with' one or other of these boys or if we were not, we pretended we were. Some of the girls actually walked down the nearby lane on Sunday afternoons for secretive meetings with their sweethearts, and with a sense of great daring and heart fluttering. And those more daring still told of meetings in the dark outside the college when the boys were supposed to be in bed.

It was all very exciting and if you had not captured a boy friend from one or other of the boys' schools by the time you were in fourth form then you were to be pitied, but you had to make sure that none of the teachers knew about these relationships, and certainly the headmistress had to be kept in the dark. It was mostly all very innocent really, and any harm that may have come of it was only in the minds of those who thought they knew best for us.

There was one teacher, however, who must have known all about those forbidden boy-girl relationships. She was the art teacher and shared her teaching between the boys' and the girls' schools. She was very young, just out of college, and to our minds, very beautiful indeed. Most of us had a crush on her. She wore up to date clothes and never seemed to wear the same ones twice. As she sat helping us with our designs we were more interested in looking at her than at what she was doing. She had beautiful eyes and we considered that she had even longer lashes than Greta Garbo, and they were her own!

Her hair was short and waved. Looking back now I think it must have resembled corrugated iron with its regular bumpy surface, but it was the mode of the day and the kiss curls she wore in the middle of her forehead must have caused raised eyebrows in the staffroom.

We followed her romance with great interest and we were all agog when she started to wear an engagement ring. It became as big an attraction to us as her eyelashes had once been. I had never seen anything like it except in the jeweller's shop window for nobody in my family wore such a beautiful ring and certainly none of the other teachers did.

I was well into my school career when she left to get married and we presented her with a cut-glass water set. I loved it all for it was not often that there were such 'happenings' in our all girls' school.

Chapter 12

I was twelve when we moved away from my grandmother's house. The seven children there were growing fast and our bedroom was the extra accommodation that my aunt, with four boys to raise, so desperately needed.

It was difficult for us to find anywhere to go at a rent we could afford, but at last we were allocated a council house that would cost only two shillings a week more than we were already paying for our two rooms. My other must have been very pleased to move away to a place of her own after those long, difficult years living in the same house as her in-laws.

But to me it was a terrible wrench for it seemed that I belonged in that house of my early childhood. However, we were not moving far away and through the years I was fortunate indeed in that I really had two homes ad could still find refuge in Granny's workroom or in the kitchen where Auntie Min always had her famous bone broth on the stove and delighted in giving me a cupful in and out to 'make you strong'. It was not much more than water really, flavoured by a stripped bone but with added salt and pepper it was comforting on a cold day and warmed my heart as well.

I did not like our new home and even my mother declared that whoever designed it should have been put up against a wall and shot. It was one of a long terrace and was all back to front. As the front doors opened on to a very narrow communal path and the only vehicular road ran along the back of the houses, everyone used the back doors which opened straight into their sculleries. The front doors were seldom opened.

As in so many council houses at that time, the lavatory was just outside the back door, and any caller to the house would be standing outside the lavatory door while any person inside the loo at that time was trapped there until the caller went away or was admitted into the scullery. Imagine the embarrassment of having to emerge from the lavatory to answer the door if nobody else was at home.

The scullery was unbelievable, with a sink and a cold tap in one corner and a washing copper for boiling clothes in the other. Between these two was a large white enamel bath, an incongruous sight in a kitchen of all places. Apparently we were not entitled to a separate bathroom and instead of bathing in front of the living room fire, as before, we now had to make sure the scullery door was locked in case of visitors, and the curtains drawn in case of peepers before taking our weekly baths. A bath more often than that would have been out of the question with all the disruption it caused.

Presumably it was considered convenient to fill the copper from the cold tap at the other end of the kitchen, light the fire under it, and then, when hot enough, dip the water into the bath. Then there was the business of cleaning out the ashes from under the copper afterwards. Small wonder that some tenants in the terrace never used their baths at all but contented themselves with a swill off at the sink, and even found the bath a useful receptacle for coal or anything else which needed a dumping place.

The only thing to be said in favour of the copper was that it made a very warm corner on the innumerable washdays in our house and then it was very pleasant to have the chair at that end of the table at mealtimes. The scullery was just big enough for dining during the week but on Sundays we always used the front room as my mother was at home all day and it was special.

Leading off from the scullery was a short dark passage that led to the pantry on one side and the coalhouse under the stairs on the other. The doors of these were so arranged that if one was open, you could not open the other, but the pantry was large and airy and the first place we aimed for when, coming home from school and no mother to greet us, we searched for a stay stomach in the form of nubbies, as we called buns, or a corner of cold pasty.

There was a small black gas cooker in the scullery but my mother preferred the coal range in the front room, the only other room downstairs. If the range was meant for cooking, why was it put in the best room when the food preparation was done in the scullery? That the food tasted better when cooked by coal fire there was no doubt, probably because my mother was not used to a gas cooker, but it was a case of preparing the food in the kitchen, baking it in the front room, and then carrying it back to the kitchen again to be served. Even when we dined in the front room the potatoes, cabbage and other vegetables had to be drained at the kitchen sink. What a performance!

I suppose the answer to all this inconvenience was that it had all been designed for economy and that working class families with low incomes were not supposed to need any more than one room in which to go through the motions of everyday living, and a scullery thrown in with a bath in it, and a cooker when people did not want fires, well... what more could anyone ask? And what could we expect for six shillings a week? Obviously, beggars could not be choosers.

We had three good bedrooms and one bed per room was indeed luxury, for two of us at least could have our own room each except for the time when we had visitors or occasional lodgers who helped to supplement the family income. But they were often very poor as well and could not afford to pay much.

The view from the house was magnificent and the best feature of that drab dwelling place, or at least it was drab when we first went there and it smelled of distemper and freshly scrubbed floors. All the walls were distempered n cream and the paintwork was dark fawn, a dreary colour that symbolised the lives of many people in those hard times. But my mother was a home maker and as time went by we found ourselves in a spotlessly clean, comfortably furnished home which though humble and often very untidy had linoleum throughout so highly polished that relatives were heard to say that you could eat your meals off the floor!

The neighbours were a mix of good and bad. Some kept themselves to themselves while others were found of what my mother called 'housing'. Some lived quiet respectable lives while others sometimes roused the neighbourhood with their husband and wife rows, especially n Saturday nights. There were often indescribably scenes of violence, sometimes necessitating the summoning of the police and foul language was an everyday occurrence. Everybody seemed to know everybody else's business and bickering between the neighbours was commonplace. After the peace of Granny's house it was so different, and the way people around me lived and the harsh realities of life seared into my sensitive soul.

There were dozens of children living in that terrace and most of them played in the road outside. By the time we went to live there I had outgrown the playing stage and spent most of my spare time doing schoolwork or private reading. I could not get enough books to read and made frequent trips to the Public Library where I enjoyed browsing through the daily newspapers before choosing books to take home.

Some of the neighbours' children were constantly knocking at doors asking for a shilling for two sixpences for the gas meter or other items such as tea or sugar that their mothers had forgotten at the shops. When they came knocking on our door I found it exasperating but I expect I was as much of nuisance as they were for I often knocked on neighbours' doors asking if they had any magazines I could read.

I had no time to playing the road, even if I had desired to do so and was such a bookworm that often when my mother spoke to me I did not hear her, so absorbed was I in my reading, "It's no good speaking to 'er," she would say, "'er old 'ead's in a book as usual."

The other children in the terrace thought I was stuck up because I did not mix with them but we did not share the same interests and one usually finds one's special friends at school. Goodness knows, I did not consider myself above them, as they thought I did. We were very poor and some of the young people around us were in far better circumstances than I, but they were not old enough perhaps to realise that a withdrawn personality does not always signify a self-opinionated one.

However, over the years the houses have been redesigned inside and are now more convenient places in which to live and from all accounts quite comfortable. The terrace has improved in many ways and is very different to when we lived there all those years ago. Most of the children too grew up and made good some of them doing very well indeed. A tough upbringing so often seems to bring out the best in people's later lives....

Chapter 14

We were very poor indeed but rather more fortunate perhaps than some of our neighbours who lived in absolute squalor. We were probably the only poor children around who had a grandmother who was forever making new clothes from old or relatives who could provide us with hand-me-down garments.

But it was hard grind for my mother and it was a rare sight indeed to see her sitting down at leisure. As well as her eight pence an hour domestic work, she took in washing. The house seemed always to smell of soapsuds or freshly ironed clothes, and on wet or dry days an indoor clothesline was a permanent fixture either for drying the clothes or airing them after that had been ironed.

She did my teachers' washing so obviously I was the only girl in the school who knew what sort of knickers they wore! They had beautiful under-garments that my mother laundered to perfection under very trying conditions. Each of the three teachers she worked for had a very large cardboard laundry box and a book in which they listed each item. Every week I would total up the amounts charged and carry the boxes, held flat, to the respective rooms or digs. There I was paid the few shillings the books showed and then called back later for the next batch of laundry. It was very hard work for a small return but two lots of laundry were enough to pay the rent; even so we were often in arrears, and then how quickly it mounted up.

When my mother first started to do the laundry, there was one item listed which was very puzzling. It was shown on the book as '1 mod vest'. We searched the box but could find no extra vest. I could not have lost it as the box was tied with string and anyway the number of items listed matched the number I had brought home. It turned out that the 'mod vest' meant 'modesty vest', a small handkerchief sized piece of silken material with lace on the top that was pinned inside a dress in order to fill up the gap left by a low 'V' neckline. Women did not display bosoms in those days, especially in school, and any hint of them had to be hidden at all costs.

As well as the teachers' laundry my mother grabbed any other chance of such work as came along. One day a fun fair came to the town and the owners wanted someone to do their washing. They said that they did not want each item costed separately but named a very generous figure for the work as a whole. It was too good a chance to be missed.

It was a mountain of dirty washing consisting of caravan curtains, loose covers as well as clothes and bed linen, all first class items. There was so much to do that even I had to help my mother with all the ironing. Normally she never let me touch the teachers' laundry in case I singed any of the elegant garments as we used flat irons heated on the stove or the gas cooker and it was difficult to judge just the right temperature.

We ironed well into the night and at last it was finished and carried to the caravans that clearly belonged to the top people of the fairground. How trusting was my mother when she was told she'd be paid after the evening's takings from the fair, and how heartbroken when she discovered that they had no intention of paying and had left the town with a string of debts behind them. The shopkeepers may have followed it up and eventually got paid but in our case it was a whole lot of work for nothing because of that moonlight flit.

My mother was not strong in body but had considerable willpower and was never known to give in easily. Indeed she did work literally until she dropped and one hard winter, having struggled on defiantly with a heavy cold, she went down with pneumonia. It was a dreadful time in our lives ad the thought that this was the illness that had killed our father must have been ever-present in our minds.

It was a nightmare of poultices, thermogene, sputum mugs and the doctor or nurse coming into the house with anxious looks on their faces. It seemed to go on forever and I had to stay away from school and more or less take over my mother's place in the home. It was a stern task indeed for a thirteen year-old in such poor circumstances and I could not have managed without the kind help of neighbours and friends. In times of trouble people rallied round to do what they could and I will never forget what they did at that particular time.

They never let us go hungry. Although in ordinary times we often ran in from school declaring that we were starving, it was not ever true and our mother was an excellent cook and managed to provide us with nourishing, inexpensive meals. And now, with outside help, we never went without either, even though some of the meals I produced left a great deal to be desired. I never showed much talent as a cook and even today I'm very aware of my shortcomings in this direction.

People brought beef broth for my sick mother and her cousins took over the teachers' washing so that we would not miss the money coming in. We had to keep a coal fire burning in the bedroom both day and night but Auntie Min was always a great one for providing a hundredweight of coal now and again and in sickness she was even more generous. Coal cost half-a-crown a bag that was a quarter of her pension, but she seldom thought of herself.

The nights were the worst for it was then that my mother coughed most and had to be helped into a sitting position so that she could breathe. It was all very frightening. Then people began to talk about 'the crisis' that meant that the time had come when she would just have to get through that particular night or it would mean the end.

A neighbour kept us company on that dreadful night for I do not think that anyone thought my mother would live through it, but miraculously that frail little woman pulled through. The district nurse and the doctor had done a good job and when it was certain that the patient was over the worst, the nurse plumped up the pillows behind her to prop her up and said briskly,
"You've been through Hell!"

And that was that but the trials and tribulations were not over and many months went by before things got back to normal once more. I often woke up in the night to hear my mother suffering a severe bout of coughing from which it seemed she could not recover and there was always the fear that the dreaded pneumonia would return.

But, after a while, she regained her health and returned to normal work as well as taking on extra as well. As she was such a good cook she used to fill in at the local hospital when the resident cook was ill or on holiday. We looked forward to these times, not fully aware of the strain it was bound to put on our mother, but we were allowed to have our midday meal in the hospital kitchen, either food that had been brought from home and cooked there or, often, any leftovers from the hospital fare.

It was fascinating to watch the matron slicing off the meat from such enormous joints that were a rare sight indeed, and then watching the plates of food going up in the lift to the floor on which the wards were situated. In the afternoon, the porter cut bread and butter for the patients and I had never seen such wafer thin slices of bread that he cut with such dexterity and which were so unlike the 'doorsteps' to which we were accustomed.

I loved going to the hospital kitchen because further along the corridor was a room where all the old newspapers and magazines were dumped and I was able to read to my heart's content. There was a hospital smell about them though which made me wonder if they were perhaps crawling with germs, and I was scared to death of the black beetles which scuttled away as I collected my reading material from that dark, underground room.

The matron was a handsome woman, regal in her uniform, and she always called my mother "Meesis". I loved the way she talked, so different from our own way of pronouncing words because she was not Cornish. She was a very good friend to my mother and provided us with many little luxuries. I liked being asked into her private sitting room that was so tastefully furnished and contained interesting ornaments and pictures.

One of the pictures really caught my eye for it was one of two Mabel Lucy Atwell-like figures, a little girl accompanied by a bashful looking little boy. He was obviously well scrubbed and was saying to the little girl,
"Kiss me kid. I'm sterilised." The matron had a very good sense of humour.

In spite of all the hard work my mother did not become ill again for some time although she had bouts of depression which were shown on her medical certificate as "Nervous Debility'. I did not know exactly what it meant now and it was a wonder that she did not succumb to a complete nervous breakdown considering the worries she had.

During her lifetime she has so far survived three major operations, one minor one and several bouts of pleurisy, the last of which resulted in many weeks of observation in a sanatorium. But she always bounced back even though she was a bundle of nerves.

"You've got to keep going," she has always said, and that is what she is still doing even at eighty, for she believes that is what keeps her alive.

Once we were all fledged and her Parish Pay stopped, the matron recommended my mother for a permanent place at the new hospital on the town's outskirts and she became well known for the cheer that she brought into the wards. She could always crack a joke or even sing a favourite hymn for a patient who requested it, and nobody took offence when she often breezed into the wards in the morning and greeted the bedridden with the words,

"You'm still yer then? You bain't daid yet!"

I don't think my mother ever read a book in the whole of her life for she never had time. I doubt that she will ever ready this one because now her sight is very poor and anyway she would not be able to sit down long enough to tackle anything as long as a book. She still thinks it's a disgrace to be found taking it easy and on hearing me come into the door will often get us quickly and busy herself putting something tidy. Old habits diehard and when you have worked hard all of your life it is very difficult to take things easy, with a clear conscience.

One day when her little flat was spotless and she was wondering what to do, she took the laces out of her shoes and washed them. Anything, rather than sit doing nothing....

Chapter 15

All the time that I was at grammar school my brother and sister were developing in their own ways. I have only vague memories of them during our mother's illness. They must have been in the house then but I do not remember them actually being there.

My brother, Ron, was not a bookworm as I was. He was more interested in practical things and though he occasionally browsed through boys' magazines which I also enjoyed, he spent most of his spare time making things. A tea chest could be bought for a few pence and with the three-ply wood and his first saw he created many ornamental pieces of work that my mother was proud to show off to relatives and friends.

Every Saturday morning he went off on a milk round into the surrounding countryside and we did not see him for the rest of the day. We had a cat in the house called Fluffy which belonged to us all, but one Saturday he returned home from his journeying around the district with his cloth cap clutched close to his chest and announced in his little gruff voice that he had his own cat in it. This was a wild little farm creature that, in an endeavour to escape, ran up the chimney but it eventually settled down and was named 'Bubbles'.

We also had a goldfish named Oscar that lived for many years in a fruit dish and survived many an escapade with the two cats around. For a short time we had a black and white mongrel dog but the neighbours used to throw buckets of water over him when he strayed into their gardens so we had to get rid of him in order to keep the peace. My mother was heartbroken about this as she was always passionately fond of animals and thought that no child should be brought up without them.

Ron was a choirboy and went regularly to the Friday practices and to both morning and evening services on Sundays. He looked very fine in his surplice and stiff, wide starched collar and my mother was so proud of him as he walked in procession down the aisle of the church. I don't know that he was much of a singer but the payment he received for his presence in church was very welcome indeed.

He left school at fourteen and was eventually apprenticed to a boot maker, becoming later a very skilled craftsman indeed. During his apprenticeship he was poorly paid and it was some time before he was on his own feet, but after serving through the Second World War in his own trade, he began to make headway and is now making quality footwear for a famous firm in London and sending it off by post each week from his workshop in Launceston. Nothing could induce him to tear up his roots and go to live in the Big City.

My sister Joyce, four years young than I, was not very interested in books either, but like my brother was certainly not unintelligent. They both did well at school, always bringing home excellent reports, but their education did not extend much beyond the three R's and practical work. Maybe this was just as well for they would not have taken kindly to the amount of bookwork I had to do both at home and at school.

Joyce showed a talent for home making that I never possessed. Her needlework was such that it was often on show at her school and at local exhibitions, and Murrumbidgee who took all the girls in the area for cookery was quick to tell me that my sister far outshone me when it came to the culinary arts.

She was a little mother to the babies in our terrace and liked to push them about in their prams and help with their baths. She adored babies and even as a small child when we lived in Westgate Street had always taken a great delight in being allowed to take out her baby cousin in his wooden pushchair. She was not allowed to go off the pavement or any further than the chestnut tree, a stone's throw up the road, but she pushed him up and down, up and down and then took further pleasure in rocking him in his little basinet when it was his bedtime.

By the time she was fourteen, my sister had become a competent young woman, much more grown up than I was. She left school to become under nurse to three children who lived with their parents in a fine country house about seven miles away. The owner of the house was an army major and he employed a cook, a butler and various other maids as well as a gamekeeper and gardeners. In other words, my sister went to work 'below stairs' and the people she worked for were always referred to as 'the gentry'.

The gardens around the house were magnificent and I loved to go there with my sister to see the strutting peacocks and the stately swans preening themselves on the lily ponds. It was all very elegant so that when I saw the bedroom that was set aside for the under nursemaid it was quite a shock. The little black iron bed and white enamel toilet accessories reminded me very much of pictures I had seen of prison cells.

But my sister was very happy with the children and received a small wage as well as her keep, and best of all she got the sort of training which was to take her later on to other far more attractive posts which were in themselves an education. To this day she is known as nanny to one of her previous charges who still visits her and was happy to become godmother to her son.

I wonder how my brother and sister would have fared under the present day education system? I fancy that they, and many more like them would have found the general curriculum of a comprehensive school less than attractive. They would have revelled in all the facilities available in the craft rooms but would have found some of the other studies, and especially the book work, very tedious indeed once they had reached fourteen.

Some children are bookish and others are not, and I am of the opinion that one reason for so much trouble in schools today is that so many of the pupils are unable to cope with their equal opportunities and only become frustrated and discontented at having to take subjects in which they see no point whatsoever.

It cannot be just poor home conditions and lack of parental control that produces problem teenagers for many children in our town at that time had poor backgrounds. Fathers came home drunk and children often ran to neighbours for protection. Life was very hard indeed buckle straps and all. But there was no serious vandalism then and I never heard of any youngsters appearing in court.

Was it because they went to schools of a reasonable size where they were not anonymous? Was it because they did not have so wide a curriculum at school that they were unable to cope with it all? How ridiculous, for example, to try to teach French to those youngsters who find written and oral expression in their own language so difficult. Small wonder that the standard of English is falling when not enough time is given to teaching it. Common Market or not, surely one's own language comes first?

But then of course there was no 'idiot box' all those years ago. What a difference TV has made to the lives of children - I am sure that the educational advantages are far outweighed by the social disadvantages for the television has taken over in so many homes to the detriment od so many youngsters. As I read recently, a quote from Professor Ivor Mills: "The kids of today are brought up on stress and are hooked on thrills."

At the time that my brother and sister were at school many of the pupils were high spirited and got into all kinds of scrapes one way and another, but things never got seriously out of hand so that people wondered where it would all end.

But then, youngsters did not have to remain at school until they were sixteen. And that says a great deal....

Chapter 16

Fortunately, I enjoyed my grammar school work in the early years, or at least most of it. There were other scholarship girls beside myself who had to struggle because of circumstances at home. Our grants helped, and the day that the District Education Officer came to the school to hand out our cash was always an occasion. Somehow it was something we kept secret from the other girls and our mysterious visits en masse to T.A.'s study were never explained to them. We signed for the money and hid it in the pockets of our coats hanging in the cloakroom before returning to our appropriate classrooms and settling down quietly without a word as to where we had been and why. Nobody asked us anything about it so I expect the other girls knew that it was something to do with being disadvantaged.

Obviously the grant did not cover all the extra expenses that were part of our education. There were hockey sticks and pads to buy, tennis racquets and many other things. It was an honour to be a member of the first hockey eleven but a bit of a headache when it came to away matches and the train or bus fares had to be found. Then there were the Christmas parties when if you were not in school uniform you could not compete with the beautiful dresses so many of the other girls wore with such flair.

But, except for the catty remarks regarding the fact that I was wearing somebody else's cast-offs or that my mother took in washing, I do not remember the girls on the whole being anything but friendly and understanding. We all had our ups and downs, found our own particular friends and had many happy times together though sadly, my grammar school days did leave an indelible mark of inferiority upon my personality.

There were no school buses then but the town boasted a small railway station and several girls travelled from outlying districts in this way, mostly at their own expense. Others who did not actually live in the town rode their bicycles, many of them for quite long distances; on wet days it was a hard job getting all their outdoor clothes dry and ready for the homeward journey.

I knew of one boy who cycled sixteen miles to school each day; he eventually won a place at a university.

Soon after we moved house I decided to attend prep sessions held at the school each weekday evening between five and seven. This was arranged so that girls wishing to do so could return after tea and do their homework in peace. There was always a teacher on duty and if we were stuck with any of our work we could get the necessary help or have access to the small reference library.

For some of us it would have been difficult to get through all the work at home where there is only one living room and the rest of the family usually around. I could not take myself off to my bedroom in the wintertime as it would have been too cold, and anyway there is a limit as to what can be done by candlelight.

There was not enough time to go home and get back to school again by five and my mother would still be at work, so as Westgate Street was nearer I always went to Granny's house for tea and Auntie Min would accompany me to the front door and secretly give me my usual three-pence.

"I do it for your father's sake," she would say kindly, almost as if she had to make some excuse for her generosity.

To supplement this amount I ran errands for a partially sighted old lady for whom my mother worked. Every Saturday morning I was sent scuttling around the various shops and sometimes I threaded her needles for her or performed other small tasks. For my labours I received three-pence a week at first and then later on a sixpenny bit. On top of this there was always a small packet of boiled sweets tucked in between the groceries, a gift especially for me from the shopkeeper.

The money thus earned usually went on magazines, school girl ones to start with and then as I got older those with more grown up content like 'Poppy's Paper' or 'Peg's Paper'. The stories in these were mostly about love but the main characters never got beyond the kissing stage and were always very pure. There were 'Agony Columns' even then and the answers to various queries clearly indicated that nice girls were meant to resist anything further than kisses and that they wouldn't be respected if they allowed any other intimacies. Sex before marriage? Definitely NOT. You must wait until you have the wedding ring on your finger....

Not all the grown-ups I knew at that time were kind although one particular woman liked to think that she was. She was apparently quite well off for she could afford a holiday bungalow beside the sea and it was put to me that maybe I would like to join her there for a holiday, along with her husband and two sons. There was a proviso, however. In order that I should get to know the family and get into their ways she thought it would be a good idea if I came to help her in her home for a bit. The summer holidays were a long way away so she knew what she was doing alright.

It seemed a wonderful idea at the time but her definition of 'help' was far different to what I had expected. For several weeks I arrived at that well-appointed house in order to take early morning tea to her husband and herself, and after that prepare breakfast before going on to school. I was no more than twelve at the time but do not remember being offered anything to eat myself.

Then, at weekends, under the guise of being taught how to cook, I found myself performing all the more menial tasks like cleaning their shoes, doing the dusting and polishing and even waiting at table. I did not mind washing the dishes as to my mind this always came into the category of helping in the house, but the jobs that woman found for me to do!

I had to call my benefactor 'Madam' and her husband 'Sir', and worst of all the two boys had to be addressed as 'Master' before their Christian names even though they were around the same age as myself.

There was no other domestic help in the house that I knew of so that the weekend jobs really did mount up, for Madam liked me to be there on Saturdays and Sundays. On top of everything else she wanted me to do, my 'employer' liked to sit at her dressing table while I did her hair for her and generally acted the part of lady's maid.

At no time did I receive any payment for what I did; the holiday by the sea was presumably going to take care of that. It was explained to me that I was not old enough to work for money and that she would be breaking the law if she paid me in this way. Maybe her conscience got the better of her, for a short while anyway, for she did give me once a string of wooden beads that she said her husband had bought for me. They were hideous and I would never have dreamed of wearing them.

On another occasion she said I could bring a friend for tea and she undoubtedly thought that this was being very charitable indeed. I invited my cousin and she likely had visions of the sort of tea we had in our own homes on Sundays, only better.

We found ourselves eating a meagre tea in the kitchen whilst Madam and her family took tea upstairs in the drawing room, the place to which I was often summoned by the ringing of one of the bells over the kitchen door.

I had not known the purpose of these bells when I first started helping in the house, but I soon found out that each one meant my presence was required in one or other of the rooms upstairs. My cousin helped me to wash the dishes after we had partaken of our frugal tea and she must have wondered what I was doing in that place, apparently working for nothing for I never told her about those awful beads.

I began to wonder myself what I was doing there. It seemed hard work for a holiday by the sea where I would obviously have to continue in my role of girl-of-all-trades. And I did not take kindly to the sniggering of the two boys as I waited at their table, for I knew it was directed at me.

The crunch came when Madam eventually produced a frilly white cap and apron, the kid worn by parlour maids in posh houses at that time. The 'lady' thought it would be nice if I garbed myself in these items, especially when answering the door. That was enough for me. I was old enough to recognise the snobbery behind all of this and promptly took off the print apron that I usually wore, left it in the kitchen and went home....

I was a dreadful child according to that woman. Fancy leaving her like that, without a word, and after she had done so much for me. I had no manners - that was the trouble, and I did not know when I was well off!

But all this was according to her, and I never wanted to set foot in a house like that again, or spend a holiday with such a dreadful woman. I would be much better off spending my holiday with my own folk my auntie's house in the country where I would not be treated as some lesser being.

When I told my aunt about this little episode in my life she said that real gentry would not have acted like that but even so there was a very sharp dividing line between the working classes and certain employers. It was a case of 'them' and 'us' and the two did not very often go together.

It was the time when country squires were regarded as being very grand indeed, almost like royalty, and when gardeners and other workers in the employ of people considered to be their 'betters', were always condescendingly called by their surnames, as if to emphasize the difference in station.

It was all summed up by the remark said to have been made by one of our local councillors when housing requirements were being considered a very long time ago,

"I don't know why any working class family wants a sitting room," he said....

And apparently, at the time there was no answer to that.

Chapter 17

The year 1931 was a very important one in my life. It was the year the boy's grammar school and Launceston College amalgamated, resulting in our own school changing its colours from black and white to green and white and a complete change of uniform. And of course it meant more expense.

We found ourselves wearing bottle green tunics and long brown cashmere stockings in winter, but the hats were rather more attractive than before though still rather peculiar. Instead of sugar bag shapes on our heads we wore something more like pudding basins with two small white buttons on the front. Prefects wore velour hats with brims which when worn at the right angle were very smart indeed. I could not wait to be a prefect but sadly I could never afford one of those coveted hats. In the summer we wore green and white gingham dresses but dispensed with the Panamas and were allowed to go hatless.

The amalgamated school was still called Launceston College and their chosen colours were royal blue and yellow. All the boys wore caps with blue and yellow stripes going around them but those who had their school colours for games could be distinguished by the addition of a large yellow tassle worn with great pride. There seemed to be a mania for stripes and the boys strutted around in their blazers looking very much like blue and yellow zebras.

This was the year when I came to the conclusion that I was a failure. It is true that I had acquired a boyfriend by then, eventually complete with tassled cap, but if it was inspiration I was looking for then this was not it. It was an on-off affair that had me at times floating on air and at others plunging into the depths of despair.

What agonies of mind I suffered because I imagined myself to be in love with this tall, shy, not very good-looking bespectacled young man. Of course my work suffered, especially when things were off between us that was very often. I was well into my fourth year at school and should have been thinking of my School Certificate examination which would be held in July the following year, but instead I had been mooning about, unable to concentrate on the school work which had come so easily before.

Now there seemed to be no point in it and who wanted to take a silly examination anyway? The original number of girls in my form had dwindled considerably. Some of the ones who had no already left to help at home on the farm or to work in their fathers' shops intended leaving soon without taking any public exams, but there was I, facing another year and more of hard slog and not showing much promise of ever being a success.

The mock examination proved my point for I did very badly indeed. I knew I had been a flash in the pan being so good at elementary school and then fizzling out when it came to the test.

The worst result was in French at which I was to score only ten marks out of a hundred. Ten marks! I was a disgrace and the Headmistress told me what she thought of me. I was like a jellyfish she said, with no backbone whatsoever. My writing had gone to the dogs and I was no showing any interest in my work. What was wrong with me, she wanted to know? I could only hang my head and offer no explanation.

She went on and on and I knew what she was saying was true. I <u>had</u> been letting things slide and it was no wonder that she was so cross with me because it looked as if I was prepared to let down all the people who had tried so hard to help me.

The 'School Certificate' was very different to the GCSE 'O' levels of today. It was divided into certain categories that demanded at least one pass in each to be sure of success. This meant that failure in French at which I had done so badly would mean complete failure of the whole examination even if I got credits in all the other subjects. French was the only foreign language we took so that we all had to get a pass in that subject or fail and take the whole examination again. There seemed to be no justice in the world....

I was not the only one who had done badly. Two of my friends, Grace and Connie, were on the carpet too but the Headmistress knew what she had to do. She had to make up for lost time - and our real understanding of the subject.

It happened that our French teacher was not one of the best I the school. I had gone through all the work without her realising that I hadn't a clue about what I was doing. My French verb book was a masterpiece of beautifully written present, past and future tenses which I could rattle off parrot fashion but I had no idea how to apply what I had learned to written exercises.

The Headmistress decided to take on the task of teaching us French and said that we'd have to go back to the very beginning and start all over again. It was going to take up a great deal of her own spare time but she was determined to try to see us through. She provided us with new files and we did page after page of homework that she marked with us in her study or during evening prep periods at school when she was on duty. She had simmered down by now and we all entered into the spirit of the thing with great zest.

Mistakes were ringed round and round by her red ink fountain pen so that they stuck out like gaping wounds on the white pages, and woe betide us if we made the same mistake twice. It became a sort of contest between the three of us to see who could do the most pages and make the fewest mistakes and, miraculously, at last I began to see through it all ad scored good marks in subsequent end of term examinations. What a wonderful woman was T.A. She need not have bothered with us but she did and it was so worthwhile.

But there were still other difficulties to overcome. We also had to get a pass in the science category and it was fault of the teacher that there was no chance at all that I would ever pass in her subjects which were chemistry and botany. I was hopeless!

There was just one other glimmer of hope; 'Housewifery' was considered to be a science subject so during my fifth year I joined a small group for a course in laundry and needlework. As it had not been an examination subject in our school before, and there was now not much time, it was very much a gamble as to whether any of us would be successful. But in my case it was absolutely essential for me to pass in this as well as in French. What hope was there? Was I ever going to be able to prove myself good enough?

We had to prepare for a written paper as well as the preparatory practical work. For the latter we had to make a nightdress, a petticoat and a pair of knickers, choosing our own colour schemes and designing our own patterns and embroidery work. Buying the material was a problem for it meant several yards and it was not cheap.

Nearly everything in the drapery shops was marked with a figure ending in eleven pence, three farthings at that time. I suppose an article priced thus looked cheaper than it really was and it was a sales gimmick. Since a farthing was rarely given as change we ended up with a few pins instead which seemed an idiotic way of doing things, but it was the general practice. You had to be good at arithmetic too in order to work out quick ways of reckoning up the prices of articles you bought with all those wretched farthings on the end of the price.

I do not remember how much the material cost but I managed to get the required amount and set to work to assemble the garments, terrified that I would spoil the material in some way in the process of cutting it out. The work had to be ready by the end of the Easter holiday, as not long after that an expert would come from the Examination Board and assesses our work.

It was what you would call a rushed job and meant hours of planning and stitching during the holiday. My head and neck ached as I bent over my work and spots danced before my eyes, but eventually I was finished. It had all been too much and one evening I was finished too, in a crumpled heap on the floor.

My mother was very worried and thought I was 'going into decline', a favourite expression in those days, though I think I had fainted as a result of bending over my needlework for too long all at one time and worrying whether I would get it completed according to schedule. However, the bottle of tonic wine which was anxiously provided for me went down well and

I'm sure had nothing to do with the fact that I was soon back to normal once more, even though I was in a constant state of anxiety.

The laundry work examination took place in the Cookery Centre on a hot day at the beginning of the summer term. Each girl had three items to launder under the eagle eye of the examiner whose name was Mrs. Savage. Well, that was a good start and we felt her name was very appropriate indeed.

We were not told which articles we would have to wash, dry and iron but the Headmistress had been secretly gathering them all together ready for the big day. We had not had many lessons beforehand and had to know precisely how much starch to use for cotton things as well as the special processes for curtain materials like cretonnes and muslins.

No talking was allowed during the examination but once we had been allocated our particular items and had got them through the wash, there was nothing to stop us having a few words outside at the clothes lines. We must have been a comic sight, all pinning out different articles with desperate looks on our faces and speaking to each other in frenzied whispers.

I have a grey crepe-de-chine blouse of Murrumbidgee's, a tea cloth and a muslin curtain to do and managed to complete my task with no catastrophes but one of my friends burnt the shape of the iron out of TAs best pink petticoat and almost burst into tears as a result. We used the flat irons heated on the coal stove and it was really difficult to estimate the correct heat.

We had brought our needlework to the Centre in large cardboard boxes and Mrs. Savage who was obviously going to leave no stitch unturned carefully examined it. I had chosen pale pink embroidered rosebuds to decorate my pale blue garments, which were bound with dainty pink ribbons. They looked quite attractive but I knew that my stitching was far from even.

We were not told then how we had done but would have to wait until late August when we would know how we had fared in all the other subjects but the examiner smiled at me as I was ironing the blouse and that was encouraging. It was such a frilly, complicated thing that I must have looked so frail and small standing at that large table wielding that flat iron over the flimsy material. And apparently she had remarked on the daintiness of my needlework so I kept my fingers crossed.

****

There could be no let-up in my other schoolwork. I had left things very late and there was now a great deal of catching up to do. In order that I could study in peace after the evening prep at school, I proceeded to Granny's house and by half past seven was sitting in solitary state in the room that used to be our own. There was no radio or TV to distract me and although I often looked longingly out of the window during those warm summer evenings and thought of the more attractive things I could be doing, I kept at it.

Our set books for the English Literature paper were 'Henry Edmond', 'Twelfth Night' and 'An Anthology of Modern Verse' and there was a lot of learning by heart to get through. To this day I remember the extracts from Shakespeare that had to be mastered and I certainly had no great love for the Immortal Bard at that time. As for Henry Esmond, well, what a bore he was and the sooner I finished with him the better. I loved poetry, but not for examination purposes, that's for sure. I go so tired that the lines blurred into one and I was weary of it all.

I had a whole file of history notes that seemed deadly dull and I found the dates difficult to memorize. I go to the state, however, when I had gone through it all so many times that I even knew in mind exactly at what stage I turned a page. It was not the best way to learn the subject for I was just cramming the facts into my head for no good purpose that I could see.

These were the subjects that had to be passed so I concentrated on them and trusted to luck for the others. I was well acquainted with The New Testament and cast that aside as well as the other less tiring things such as maths and art, which could be prepared during normal school hours.

****

And so the final day of reckoning arrived and we sat at our desks for two dreadful weeks, most of us trying to prove that we did have some brains in our silly little heads. I remember the smell of the wisteria drifting through the open window as I struggled with all the question papers and thought dismally of the future. The number in the examination room varied but I think there were never more than twelve of us in it at one time and it was interesting to note that most of us were scholarship girls for we were the ones who were expected to show that our free education was justified.

It was unfortunate for me that the geography paper was set for the first day. It was my weakest subject now and I knew that I had done badly. There seemed to be no point in taking the other subjects since I had nothing else to offer in that vital category except housewifery and of one of those entered expected to pass in that. And there was still a further section to get done before even that could be got out of the way.

It was not enough to have produced the three garments: we still had to prove that we could concoct patterns under examination conditions and do the written paper on laundry work. Most of that was, I suppose, common sense but what are you supposed to do with a man's very paint-stained and greasy overalls? My first instinct was to say, "Throw them away!" but instead I decided the best things to do would be to soak them in a bucket of petrol before washing them in very hot soapy water and then rinsing as many times as necessary to get rid of the smell. Whether it was the correct procedure or not, I scarcely had time to think for there were other, equally perplexing problems with which I had to deal.

And then, at long last, the exams were over and we would soon be enjoying the summer holidays. What bliss! What heavenly bliss after what had seemed an eternity of scholastic slavery. Now I could play tennis, swim, cycle to the seaside on a borrowed bicycle and go on breaking my heart over the boy with the tasseled cap.

Love was not, as far as I was concerned, 'the sweetest thing'....

Chapter 18

If you wanted to know the result of the examination as soon as it came out you ordered the 'Daily Telegraph' and prayed that your name would be in it on the day that it arrived. Or, if you were like me, you tried to forget about the whole thing and pretended that you couldn't care less what happened anyway.

So it was that on that particular day I decided to stay in bed. There would be no newspaper plopping through our letterbox and I certainly wasn't going to the library to find out what I already knew. Instead I buried my head in the bedclothes and felt sorry for myself.

I was just drifting off into blissful forgetfulness when I heard the back door burst open and someone was rushing up the stairs. It was my mother with 'The Telegraph' in her hand and the astonishing news that my name was in it. She had gone to the hospital to work while the cook was on holiday and Matron had seen the results and given her permission to come home and tell me.

I just could not believe it. How could it be possible when I had no science to offer with any sort of confidence? The answer came the next day on the postcard sent to each of us by T.A. and giving the detailed result of each subject. I had gained credits in French and art and had scraped through in everything else except geography. I had passed my School Certificate because I had managed a scrape in housewifery and the unexpected had happened.

It was almost laughable. I had spent five years at grammar school and all that time our home had resembled a small laundry. I had regularly carried the boxes containing the teachers' washing to and fro and had often done my homework as my mother labored at the washtub or ironing board. There were always clothes hanging over our heads in both downstairs rooms and I remembered the time when we had done all that ironing for the fairground people for no payment. Now, here was payment indeed, for I must have learned something from my mother about laundry work and had obviously inherited some of the skill my grandmother possessed when it came to needlework.

It was marvellous, for if I had failed in just that one subject my name would not have appeared among the successful candidates and the slog would have to begin all over again. It was compensation indeed for the times I had been sneered at because my mother took in washing and I had been made to feel so inferior. And French to.... A credit. What would have happened if T.A. had not taken me in tow? I shudder to think of it.

It did not take me long to present myself to the house in Westgate Street. Auntie Min had promised me a school blazer if I passed the examination and in no time at all I was in the shop and trying on one of those coveted garments.

In all the excitement, I had seen only my own name in the paper, alphabetically the first on the list, and had not thought to look any further to see how my friends had done. During the days that followed I discovered why poor Grace had not obtained her School Cert; she had not passed in Housewifery because apparently her needlework had let her down, but she was determined to become a teacher, got her certificate at the second attempt and went on to carve out a very successful career for herself. She never married and was a well-loved teacher for over forty years. And just to prove that there is not much to be said for the examination, she later excelled at needlework, making it her special teaching subject.

And Connie? Well she did not take any of the examinations for in spite of the extra work she was not considered up to standard. Her aunt, the District Nurse who had pulled my mother through pneumonia met me in the street after the results were known and really cut me down to size,
"Hmmm," she said with an exaggerated air, "It looks as if they could have got Con through, after all." It did not matter. Con

went on to a nursery training school and she too chose a career rather than marriage.

****

And that brings me to the question of what I was going to do regarding a career. Those of us who passed the examination were considered to be successes, but the certificates presented to us so grandly at the annual prize giving were certainly not passports to instant employment. This was only the beginning.

I had got my Cambridge School Certificate and I am sure that some of my relatives had visions of me actually going off to Cambridge and ending up with a string of letters after my name. Little did they know how limited was my scholastic ability! What happened was that I went back to school in September with not a clue as to what I would then do.

T.A. decided that there was only one possible career, which would offer me an immediate living and not necessitate two or three years' training, so she suggested that I should work for a civil service examination. Oh no! Not again! The very thought of it left me cold. But she outlined what was involved and before long I was working on a skeleton timetable of

English, French and maths and in between she taught me typing.

What a splendid woman she was. And to think that I had once been so terrified of her. Even so I was still very much in awe of her, even though I was considered to be her favourite and could do more or less what I liked. I think she too felt sorry for me and I was just another unfortunate that she could take under her wing.

She thought it would help me if I took a correspondence course in addition to the work I did at school and which would further prepare me for the civil service exam. There was of course the question of fees, but I was not to worry she said as she would take care of those things herself. It was extraordinary that she would single me out for help in this way and soon I was working regularly through the many exercises sent to me by post from St George's College.

Meanwhile, I was enjoying school again and feeling much more relaxed. I had won my school colours in hockey, swimming and P.T. and could now take part in these activities to my heart's content. I spent a lot of time at the swimming bath. I won the school cup both that year and the following one and it was said that I was like a fish in the water. Sadly it could have only been a minnow for physically I was a late developer and a very poor specimen; I envied the other girls with their beautiful figures and super confidence.

I was also a prefect and everything seemed to be going my way. All the same I still suffered bouts of depression when I thought of myself as 'Patience on a monument, smiling at grief'. I had no business to feel the least bit unhappy but I suppose it was all part of the wretched business of growing up. I did not want to grow up, that was the trouble, and I felt that I would like to stay on at school forever....

****

I was just sixteen years old but dressed in my school uniform both in summer and winter I could have passed for twelve, being just over five feet tall and weighing only a little over seven stones. There was certainly no need for me to wear a bra for I had no shape whatsoever above my waistline except for that of a very flat pancake. And worst of all, I had acne.

Those who have never experienced this disfiguring complaint can have no idea of the misery suffered by those so afflicted, and it was no help to be told it was a teenage problem which would disappear by the time I was twenty-one. All those years ... How could I endure it? I wore my hair in a fringe, but since that was like a greasy comb stretched across my forehead it only aggravated the trouble and I always felt dirty even though I was forever washing my face.

The matron at the hospital even arranged for me to see a doctor, so sorry was she for me in my pitiful state, but no amount of treatment made any difference. How I envied my friends with their fresh complexions and burnished hair. It seemed that I was the only one with a face that should be kept hidden and probably accounted for the fact that I blushed to the roots of my hair at the slightest embarrassment.

But, life had to go on and when I was not in the throes of self-pity, I was enjoying the little extras, which were part of my school life at that time.

T.A. was a member of the Amateur Dramatic Society and enjoyed taking us for drama as an after-school activity. I was Maria in 'Twelfth Night', Portia in 'The Merchant of Venice' and the princess in 'The Princess and the Woodcutter'. It was surprising how a layer of make-up could cover up one's complexion even to the extent of making one's face quite presentable, but I don't suppose it did my acne any good.

Once, when T.A. was taking the part of Elizabeth in 'The Barretts of Wimpole Street' a friend and I spent many hours in the school attic re-upholstering the couch she was to recline on during the play in the town hall.

That woman could turn her hand to anything and supervised the work we did on the couch demanding absolute perfection. Unfortunately, during rehearsal she found that one of the springs was decidedly uncomfortable and as she had to sit on it for so long there was nothing for it but to take the whole thing apart and begin all over again. As a reward for our labours we were given free tickets for the play although T.A. said she thought it was rather an adult play for us to understand and she did wonder if we should see it. Considering that we had read the difficult 'Henry Esmond' so recently and the complications of his life it was difficult to understand her concern, for we enjoyed the play immensely and understood it. And those love scenes between Elizabeth and Robert - was it really our Headmistress up there on the stage actually kissing that handsome young man from the insurance office?

At another time she decided it would be a good idea if we tried our hands at making loose chair covers, frills and all. It was all part of our education she said, and there was no doubt that she undertook to teach us many things outside the school curriculum once we had our Cambridge exams out of the way.

She even let us use her own electric sewing machine that at that time was such a luxury.

I could not afford to neglect my other work though and made frequent visits to the library for the numerous classics listed by my correspondence course tutor. I enjoyed the drama of 'Macbeth' and the sadness of 'Jane Eyre'. Indeed I seemed to wallow in melancholy. I liked sad books, sad songs and sad films. Greta Garbo in 'Camille was something I could have watched over and over again and Al Jolson singing 'Sonny Boy' - well, that was something else....

The 'Talkies' had recently come to our town and films like 'All Quiet on the Western Front', 'Journey's End' and 'Hell's Angels', Ben Lyon and all, were the ones which drew the crowds and if you went to the cinema with a boyfriend and sat in the best seats which cost nine pence, then you really were somebody. I, alas, was never in that enviable company.

There was no need for the cinema pianist any more, or even the phantom orchestra which later accompanied silent films, We had actors and actresses actually talking and we began to come out with Americanisms like, "Oh yeah," and the now common, "O.K."

I rather fancied myself as a mimic and often entertained my friends to a takeoff of Janet Gaynor. I would start off by saying in the little girl voice of that famous star,

"I'm going to have a little party tonight," and then would follow with the voice of Greta Garbo saying that she couldn't come because she wanted, "to be a-lone'. Florence Desmond was a great impersonator at that time and I used to copy her.

It was odd that while I always felt so inferior and self-conscious, at the same time I was such a little exhibitionist. Many times I was told that I should go on the stage and there is no doubt that I found everything to do with the entertainment business, very fascinating indeed. But, when actually on the stage in school plays or in the choir, I always felt ill to the point of collapse. Simply to walk on the stage to receive a cup or certificate was enough to have my heart racing and my legs feeling like jelly.

And that is exactly how I felt when I went to Plymouth to take The Civil Service Examination.

Chapter 19

I was almost seventeen when I set off by train to face that awful examination. I was going to stay with relatives and although Plymouth was only twenty-six miles away, it seemed that I was going to the other end of the world. There I was on the station platform not really looking or feeling myself. I had had my haired permed at Auntie Min's expense but came to the conclusion that it had not been worth the trouble or the money. I resemble a poodle dog with my short hair all crimped and curled and I had spent all those hours at the hairdresser's hitched up to the ceiling it seemed, with all those electrical gadgets.

In my suitcase I had two dresses which had been passed on to me by the art teacher and examination or not, I was going to look very smart in those garments which Granny had altered to fit my smaller figure. I had very few clothes in those days and can remember those I had then, and for several years following, to the minutest details, as well as the berets which I wore perched to one side over my head in the style of the day.

A friend was at the station to wave me goodbye, and Charles Causley, now the famous Cornish poet, came along to wish me luck. He was interested in all things educational and I knew him because I had once belonged to his concert party that had been known as 'The Frivolous Five', nerves and all!

The examination was a frightening affair and I was glad when it was all over. There were hundreds of candidates there beside myself for to get into the Civil Service at that time was very competitive indeed and the two girls who had previously passed from our school had got us all a day's holiday in celebration of their success.

The French oral test was the worst of all for when I presented myself to the examiner I became completely tongue-tied and he was clearly very impatient with me, at one stage not even bothering to hide his exasperation at having to deal with such a bird brain.

The English paper was not too bad and I could answer all the questions but the maths completely floored me. We had not done trigonometry at school and the work done through the correspondence course had clearly not been sufficient. This time I really knew that there was no miracle likely to happen and that I was going to be a complete failure.

When it was all over I stayed on in Plymouth for a few weeks and tried to put the whole things out of my mind. T.A., Launceston and all the people who had helped me seemed so far away and there were many interesting things to occupy me in such a fascinating city.

I enjoyed riding about in the tramcars and visiting places of historical interest like The Hoe, the Barbican and the museum. And then of course, there was Woolworth's and all those wonderful things that never cost more than sixpence. The store smelled of chocolate and the girls behind the counters were so sophisticated with their pencilled eyebrows and crimson cupid-bow lips. The other shops, too, were places of wonder and always had very smart assistants who called their lady customers 'Modom'.

The evenings were the best of all. There was floodlight bathing near the Hoe and fairy lights all around which, to a simple country girl like myself, seemed like something out of a Hollywood film. I went to The Gaumont Cinema to see films such as 'The White Sister', 'The sign of the Cross' and '42nd Street' and to walk on those plush carpets and actually witness the organist coming up out of the floor, well if it had not been for that wretched examination, I really would have been in seventh heaven.

One evening I was taken to see 'Bitter Sweet' at the Royal Theatre and what and experience that was. Except for the amateur productions at home I had never seen anything like it and it was all so magnificent and made me cry, especially the sad rendition of, 'I'll See You Again'.

And there was a wireless set in the house where I was staying and I used to love wearing the headphone the like of which I had never seen before.

The time went very quickly indeed and I returned home feeling very unhappy but at the same time looking forward to seeing my friends again and telling them all about my experiences. I felt very important and even the boy in his tasseled cap was glad to have me back. But as usual his interest did not last long and the heartbreak continued....

****

The result of the examination would not be known until December so I went back to school to continue with the subject considered helpful should I pass but I knew, really knew, that there was no chance of that. I was happy to be back but still very depressed. I did not want to grow up. There I was, almost at the age when my mother had got married and I was still in a gymslip and very much a schoolgirl.

Many girls my age were the bright young things of the town, often referred to in those days as 'flappers'. They wore fashionable clothes and went to dances. I had been to a few but had been such a wallflower that I soon decided that this sort of thing was not for me. The cheap satin shoes that I wore for those occasions were too uncomfortable for me to walk in, let alone dance and I wobbled about on those high heels like a pygmy on stilts.

I never owned a dance dress in the whole of my life but I do not think I missed anything for I never took to being wheeled around the shiny floors by someone I didn't know and who make stilted conversation above the blare of the music. I much preferred the country dancing we did at school and loved The Floral Dance when on May Day we danced through the streets accompanied by the town band and the clapping of the onlookers. It was much more wholesome than the atmosphere of the sixpenny hop.

The on-off relationship with the boyfriend continued. It was a very sad affair punctuated by crushes on one or two other schoolboys who popped into my life and promptly out again - and no wonder. It must have been the indifference of my first love that appealed to me but it was a very strange affair indeed, lasting spasmodically over almost five years....

All it amounted to was an occasional walk in the evening with a hurried peck, which was supposed to be a kiss at the end of it. On some occasions he might put his arm around my waist as we walked and talked, mostly about school experiences, but for all that when, for some reason or another we were not seeing each other, there were nails in my heart and I was at enmity with the world.

All our meetings went on in secret of course and the headmistress was not supposed to know anything about them. Had I met her on one of those 'romantic' evening walks I think I would have died but she must have known that girls of our age were not likely to content ourselves with only female company and most likely turned a blind eye. And why not? We were not doing any harm except breaking our hearts into tiny pieces. Or at least some of us were....

We were given no sex education in those days and undoubtedly picked up a great deal of the wrong sort of information but there were no schoolgirl pregnancies or gymslip abortions either. Not in our school anyway. Most of my friends would not have known what the word 'abortion' meant and schoolgirls acted like schoolgirls. Mercifully they did not have to cope with the over-emphasized side of sexual affairs, so much a feature of today's mass media.

****

And when the results of an examination are published and you have failed miserably, then what do you do? This time there was no mother galloping up the stairs to tell me I had passed.

Instead a letter came simply informing me that I had not been successful and accompanied by the relevant details.

I dreaded telling T.A. the news after she had been so good to me and so sure that I would pass. I went timidly to her study with a trembling voice told her the news. I thought she was going to weep too but instead she gathered me into her arms, told me not to worry and said consolingly that something else would turn up.

There followed several weeks of sheer misery....

Chapter 20

What a selfish little beast I was, for my failure must have been far worse for my mother than it was for me. There she was, slaving away, sometimes until long after midnight, and with a seventeen year-old daughter not yet earning her won living. Small wonder that she often lost patience with me and told me how useless I was. Her words seared into my heart and only made me even more morose and withdrawn.

The year was 1933 and it was hard indeed to find a job at that time. Remembering my own tortured state of mind it is not difficult to understand the attitudes of young people today, thousands of them, who are unable to find employment. It did not help either when I was told by well-meaning folk that I ought to be ashamed of myself, still going to school and keeping my mother poor.

I was at enmity with the world most of the time and took it out on those I loved best; or that is how it must have seemed to them. Days would go by and I would not speak to anybody at home, or if I did it was only to utter some scathing remark or to answer with a curt yes or no to any question put to me. I hated my sister who was such a little mother in the house and so happy.

I even went out of my way to show the folks at Westgate that I didn't care a hoot about any of them. What was the good of anything? I knew that Granny and Auntie Min disapproved of make-up so for a time I deliberately took to going to see them at weekends with my face daubed with paint and powder, resembling no doubt, a circus clown. How incongruous I must have looked with my child's body and painted face, but they must have understood for they made no comment, not even a "What sense!" out of Auntie Min.

I joined in all sorts of madcap adventures with my friends, smoking on the trains that took us to hockey matches against other schools and being violently sick in the process and, sometimes, going to my beloved public library gleefully tormenting the old librarian with idiotic pranks.

Fortunately it was all just a silly phase, which did not last very long. I think I was just pretending to be somebody else - anybody but the 'me' who was so desperately unhappy. 'Sweet seventeen' indeed. As far as I was concerned it was nothing of the sort....

I had always kept diaries that showed briefly the events of the day but now, with more time on my hands, I began a more details account of the happenings in my life. It seemed that getting it down on paper was a way of coming to terms with myself and getting to realise just how fortunate I was.

We used to sing a song at school that ran:

'Forty years in when far and asunder,
Parted are those who are singing today,
When you look back and forgetfully wonder
What you were like in your work and your play,
Then it will be that will often come o'er you
Glimpses of notes like the catch of a song,
Visions of girlhood shall float then before you,
Echoes of Dreamland shall bear them along.'

Forty years on seemed more than a lifetime away, but with those words in my mind I started scribbling, never dreaming at that time then even more than forty years on I would be writing about those 'visions of girlhood' in a book for my grandchildren.

****

I was only really happy when I was at school, helping with all the clerical duties involved in its administration and helping in the kindergarten, which had recently been established in our building. This was a very small private school for both boys and girls up to eleven. They were housed in one classroom only with one teacher, for there were no more than about twenty children in all.

Meanwhile I continued with my typing exercises and the bookkeeping, which I enjoyed very much. I tried to learn shorthand but did not get on very well with the teacher. Auntie Min paid for these private lessons and for the books but it was no good and I gave it up eventually in despair. I did not tell anybody that it was largely because of the little man who taught me. He really gave me the creeps for he was very fond of putting his arm around me when I was struggling with Pitman and I didn't like him breathing on me the way he did.

I tried for several jobs but either I was considered too immature in appearance or the wages offered were too poor. I could have gone to Plymouth to work in one of the big stores but as I had no experience a premium was asked and even after three years I would have been earning only ten shillings a wee and I could not keep myself on that away from home.

It was the same when I applied for a job as a cashier at a local grocer's shop. I was offered five shillings for the first year, seven and six the next and finally that same sum of ten shillings for the third year. After that they would undoubtedly be looking for someone else to count as an apprentice in that desk as there was little chance that I would be kept on once the three years had been completed and I would be expecting more money.

It was all very discouraging and there seemed no point in having a good education. My mother was very bitter about it all, having worked so hard and apparently for nothing. Sometimes, in utter despair, she told me that I needn't think I could lead a lady's life. I would have to work the same as she had. She reckoned that all that bookwork was no good to anybody.

Obviously I was in no position to pick and choose what I was going to do in the way of work and the job at the grocer's was better than nothing, especially living at home, so I went to T.A. and told her that I was fixed up. She was delighted but when I told her the details she nearly exploded! She would not see me wasted in that way, she said. Five shillings a week indeed.... She would rather pay me that amount herself.... And that is exactly what she did, for by now she had other ideas about what my career should be.

She said that from her own observations and from reports she had received from the kindergarten teacher, she knew that I ought to go in for teaching and what did I think about that? I loved everything to do with school and the idea of becoming a teacher appealed to me very much although I had not even been considering it until she put the idea to me. I had never considered myself good enough and now here was T.A. still trying to set me on course and proving that she had more faith in me than I had in myself.

I could not begin probationary teaching until I was eighteen at least and because of my birth date I would be three months over that age when I started my training. It seemed a very long time to remain a burden on my mother but it would have been no different had I become a cashier at the grocer's shop, for every Thursday, over a period of almost a year, that generous woman to whom I owe so much, paid me five shillings a week out of her own pocket and I could look forward to the future with more confidence.

T.A. used to hand me the money in an envelope and always referred to it as my earnings for she explained to me that she did not know how she would manage all the clerical work on her own, and anyway I was so useful in the kindergarten. Of course she was just being kind. She could have coped perfectly well without my help as she had done all along, and there were other girls as well as myself who could have helped with the younger children.

I still collected my grant at the end of each term, the same amount as when I started at the school, so in effect I was better off than if I had gone out to work. A lucky girl indeed. It did not help me to grow up, however, for I still preferred to wear my school uniform which did not single me out as being one of the poorer brethren and obviously the silly make-up phase had been quite out of keeping with the real me.

There was too another young man who came into my life during and off' period with my other heartthrob and this gave me just a little more confidence in myself. Not that I was bowled over by him, far from it, but the fact that he was a university student of divinity and actually enjoyed my company made me feel that I wasn't quite the freak that I had thought myself to be after all. My friends were frankly astonished that I should have found such an elite companion, and with such a cultivated accent too. I delighted in their incredulity.

He was an outdoor type and quite good-looking. We swam, cycled, climbed the Cornish tors and played tennis. And he called me darling! That made me squirm really for it was so artificial, but nobody had ever called me that before and it all became part of the act. He also carried an umbrella that I found a bit cissy and not a bit like my rugby-playing ex-boyfriend. But, he was chivalrous and even invited me to his home for tea.

I obviously did not know anything about refined behaviour. I went up to the bathroom before tea and as it was a hot day, I removed my ankle socks and came into the drawing room with the apparently offending things in my hand wondering where I should put them. "How indelicate," he said when he saw them, so I just stuffed them behind a cushion until it was time for me to go home.

One day we went to Plymouth by train, umbrella and all, and actually sat down to a five-course lunch in a posh restaurant. Or that is what he called it, I preferred to call it 'dinner' for it was in the middle of the day and at home we never ate dinner in the evening. But I had never been in such refined company before. Nor had I ever eaten grapefruit. I looked at my portion in dismay and wondered how I was supposed to eat it for there was such an array of cutlery on the table that it was very bewildering. It was a case of 'follow the leader'.

Afterwards, he asked me if I had enjoyed the Madeira and not knowing that he was referring to the wine, I said stupidly,
"Oh I didn't know we had any cake." And then, when he suggested I might like to go and powder my nose I asked innocently, "Oh is it shining?"

What an idiot I was but I expect he found it all very amusing and enjoyed showing of his know-how. I went to the railway station to see him off after the summer vacation.
"Write to me!" he shouted as the train was moving off, "Jesus will find me."

Onlookers would not have known that he was a student at Jesus College and must have thought they were seeing a young man about to be saved by religion. What a laugh!

And that is what that little episode in my life was: just a laugh. Hilarious really, for I knew that I was just a vacation filler even though he said he had fallen for my blue eyes and that I reminded him of Laura la Plante, his favourite film star. It was an insult to that lovely lady and I didn't believe a word of it, so no hearts were broken when it was all over and he went on to become a minister of religion and I looked forward to my career as a teacher.

****

My last months at school were very enjoyable. I had come out of the doldrums for things were straightening out and the future was not now looming ahead with uncertainty. How fortunate I was for there had been more than one fairy godmother in my life to help transform the 'rags' into 'riches' - not riches in the usual sense of the word but something more valuable, for it had to do with the quality of life.

And so I began to grow up....

PART TWO

Chapter 21

In order to be accepted as a Probationary Teacher I had first to be interviewed by the County Secretary for Education and this took place in the presence of the District Education Officer as well as the Attendance Officer. There were three other applicants beside myself and there were not places for all of us so we had to do some tests to show what aptitude we had for teaching.

I had a wonderful testimonial from T.A. but felt very shaky when I was asked to draw a map of Cornwall and put in various towns and rivers. What a duffer I was. I put Newquay, that well-known seaside resort, inland and the River Tamar, only half a mile from where I lived and the boundary between Devon and Cornwall appeared on the map as a wobbly line, miles from where it should be.

It's a good job that the three gentlemen present had soft hearts and understood my difficulties for they decided, geography or not, that I was worth a gamble and on a very cold day in January I began my probationary course.

I began my training in a small, two-teacher school at the other end of the town and on top of a steep hill. It was quite a walk for anybody but more often than not I ran most of the way down one hill and partway up the other, eager to begin the day's work and learn all I could about teaching.

Everyone who wanted to become a teacher had first to do a probationary stint and at its end could either go on to become uncertificated or proceed to the training college in Truro for a further two years of more intensive training and then end up as a fully trained certificated teacher.

It was clear that I would never be able to afford college training, even with a grant, so I settled for the less remunerative, uncertificated category and meanwhile was paid a small salary whilst training. It was like a fortune to me and I could contribute more substantially towards the family income than at one time seemed possible.

The Head Teacher really put me through my paces for she was very thorough in everything she did and was obviously determined to mould me into her own image.
"Always be ready for each lesson," she said, "and never, ever let the children see you slacking." Not that I would ever have dared to slacken anyway, but it was good advice that I never forgot.

"Always keep a straight face," she went on, "Even when the situation is comic but there has been some misdemeanour. Never let the children know that you find it amusing."

I found it very difficult sometimes to follow this advice and remember the tubby four-year old boy, who strutted into the classroom during one playtime and said indignantly,
"'ee peed in my ear, 'ee did."

I found it hard to suppress a giggle as I pictured the scene but Miss Scoble's very straight face was all I needed to make me endeavour to look like an outraged teacher, aghast at such behaviour.

Probationary training was hard work but it had its similar lighter moments when we could have a good laugh together. Like when I left the room to go to the lavatory and found myself shut in that foul-smelling primitive little place. No amount of fiddling at the lock with a hairgrip had any effect and I suffered the indignity of having to shout at the top of my lungs when the children came out to play, in order to obtain my release.

Children had 'reversal' problems then, as now, when it came to spelling and one note picked up from a small boy to his girl friend ran,

"Do you love me? Yes or on?" The notes that parents wrote were often good for a laugh, like the one I was told about which was to excuse a boy's absence from school,
"Johnny can't come because he keeps going. When he stops going he can come." I expect the spelling and the punctuation were not quite like that but at least the teacher gathered that the boy 'had the runs' and could not possibly attend school.

Miss Scoble told me many other such tales and had a delightful sense of humour. She became a very good friend and was more than an ordinary tutor to me. I spent many an evening with her in her comfortably furnished schoolhouse when she used to teach me basket making and other handicrafts which would be useful t me later on.

I was till 'on' and 'off' with the reluctant boyfriend by then at university and when he came home he would join me on my visits to Miss Scoble who so enjoyed the company of young people like us.

After about five months I went to another school to complete my six months training and in order to gain experience with older children, the ones so far having been only up to eleven. It was a terrifying experience standing in front of class of thirteen to fourteen year olds, some bigger than myself, giving a lesson while the forbidding Head Teacher stood by. As I wrote on the blackboard the chalk almost dissolved into my fingers, so damp were my hands with the fear within me.

Each lesson had to be well-prepared and written out as regards aim and procedure. This, accompanied by all the necessary notes was handed to the Head teacher before the start of each of my pathetic gabblings as I tried to put the facts across and then, afterwards, it was all marked and a suitable comment as to my performance was added underneath. Every lesson was an ordeal to me and I cannot imagine that any of the youngsters gained very much from my nervous dishing out of knowledge. And with the Head there, not one of them could get away from listening to my outpourings and must have thought it was some sort of punishment! Discipline was such that I would not have dared to sit down in his presence unless invited to do so, and even in summer the bare legs of a teacher, or even bare arms, were not allowed in the classroom. You had always to set a good example and remember your duty to the children I was told.

Good advice indeed, but there was more to come.... A friend of mine who was also a teacher had recently acquired a motorbike. Well, whatever next? A woman riding a motorbike! I ought to have known that it would not have been considered ladylike to ride pillion on that enormous machine.

Nevertheless, one Sunday afternoon my friend and I took ourselves off to the moors just outside the town.

We took our bathing costumes with us and dared to sunbathe on the short moorland grass verging on the main road to the coast. As we were lying there enjoying the sunshine an A.A. man came along on his motorbike and since he knew us both, stopped to have a chat. So, there we were, two young things in bathing suits and actually talking to a man.... Disgraceful!

I heard about it the next day, and no mistake. The Head had been passing in his car on the way to the seaside when he had seen us so innocently engaged in conversation with that very nice, harmless man, and oh boy!

Didn't I know that I was a teacher now, and must act accordingly? What if any of the parents had seen us by the wayside, exposed in this way? On no account must I let this sort of thing happen again.

I listened to him going on and on and felt a laugh twitching at the corners of my mouth even though at the same time almost trembling at his wrath. It all seemed so ridiculous and he looked so outraged with his eyebrows going up and down.

"We weren't doing anything wrong," I said meekly and he knew very well we weren't for all his going on about it. But even Head Teachers are human, however fierce they may appear to be, for as I took my leave of him I fancy I saw a little twinkle in his eye.

He certainly didn't allow the incident to influence him when he wrote my testimonial for it was couched in such terms as to make me almost believe that I was God's gift to the teaching profession! Perhaps my lessons were not as bad as I thought them after all.

Miss Scoble had begged me to consider going to a training college but it was absolutely out of the question. She outlined the help I could get and emphasized the difference it would make to my career, but my mind was made up. I would no longer be a burden on my mother after all the sacrifices she had already made and so I set about applying for a post as an uncertificated teacher.

The District Education Officer proved himself to be a very good friend, taking me in his car to various interviews and counselling me as to what I should answer to the questions put to me by the managers. And so it was that I was appointed as assistant teacher in a village school about sixteen miles away and my career was really about to begin.

I would have to live away from home of course and my mother must have sighed with relief as she stood on the railway platform and watched me gradually disappearing out of sight as I waved to her from the carriage window. She had looked forward to the day when at last I would be earning my own living and off her hands and had often derided me in all the frustration of being the mother of such an awkward daughter, but she loved me really, even though at times I had doubted it. There were tears in her eyes as I took my leave of her and alone in my carriage and with all the struggles behind me, I too felt the tears welling up in my eyes....

Chapter 22

Otterham Council School was set in a hamlet that seemed to be in the middle of nowhere. There were three classrooms, three teachers and round about sixty pupils up to the age of fourteen. Their homes were scattered over a wide area and many of them had very long distances to walk to school.

I found lodgings about one and a half miles from the school and in such an exposed moorland area it was very rough in winter but pleasant enough in summer as it was only a few miles to the beautiful Cornish coast. I lived with the infants' teacher's family. Her widowed mother had a smallholding and accommodated visitors to the West Country in the summer months.

It was all very friendly and homely but I would not have gone to live in the depths of the countryside from choice for it was a very narrow existence indeed. There were only a few houses scattered around the bungalow where I lived and except for the village telephone exchange which was housed in the front room we seemed to be completely cut off from the outside world and the summer visitors must have thought that we lived at the back of beyond.

There was very little to do in the evenings except to immerse myself in my schoolwork and an oil lamp has lost its magic when you have to write by its inadequate light. Water was pumped up from a well and the lavatory, complete with newspaper, was some distance down the garden path, reminiscent of the days I spent in the country as a small child. There was a rather more sophisticated 'small room' in the wooden bungalow but this was reserved for the summer visitors and not intended for the normal household.

By present day standards the school was poorly equipped and any extras were usually obtained by our own efforts and not from generous county grants. It took two school concerts and much frenzied activity to produce enough money to provide a sewing machine and later on a gramophone and records so that I could teach country dancing.

****

I taught the middle class of eight to eleven-year olds. There were never more than sixteen children in my class but the range of ability was enormous. During the three years I was at the school there were always two or three children at the bottom of the group who had severe learning difficulties. In those days they were labelled M.D., which meant 'Mentally Deficient', and it never occurred to anyone that much could be done for them. I, in my inexperience, went along with that view but thank goodness we think differently nowadays. How dared we think that we could do nothing for those poor little souls! When I think about it now I almost hang my head in shame but I can find some consolation in the fact that some of them at any rate knew how to make money when they left school and were very likely better off eventually than I was.

It was a good thing that I was Cornish myself otherwise I would never have understood what many of the children said to me. I had not been in the school long when a boy came running into the classroom one playtime and announced,
"Eggar Dawe 'aived some mud at me an' 'it me in the chacks."

He had dirt on his face to prove what he said so I suppose that little bit of Cornish wouldn't have been too difficult to translate but it was no easy task trying to get those children to write good English. How do you begin to correct such oral outbursts as, "Yer. You don't do it like that that there. You do it like this yer yer."

Written compositions were a joy to read in some respects but were generally sadly lacking in imagination. It was not surprising really as so many of the children lived repetitious lives and had so little outside experience on which to draw. Very few of their parents had cars and travel did not extend much further than school for some of them.

One boy in the school always ended his compositions with, "...and I took off my boots and went to bed." No matter what was the content of his composition the teacher could always be sure of that same ending every time. In one 'adventure' that he wrote, he told of a picnic on the cliffs when he fell off and got drowned. All the children in the school contributed towards a wreath for him and were all crying at his funeral. There he was, presumably lying in his coffin, but he still managed to take off his boots and go to bed.

Every morning after prayers and scripture we had P.T. or rather an apology for it. The only equipment we had comprised a box of bean bags, a few skipping ropes and some large balls. If the weather was fine, we could perform in the playground but if wet, we still had to do some sort of drill in the classroom between the desks.

Outside nearly everything was done in lines with an appropriate coloured braid to show which one the children joined. My class ran on the spot, did astride jumping or various movements from a knee bend position and every so often the county supervisor came to make sure that we were doing what was laid down in the handbook of set pieces.

The sessions I took in the playground must have resembled scenes out of 'Dad's Army' with me every bit as officious and comic as Captain Mainwaring,
"Hands on hips - place!"
"Running on the spot - begin!"
"Heels – raise!"
"Knees full bend!"
"Hands in front of your feet - place!"
"Into prone position - jump!"

My voice rang out in the playground punctuated every now and then by a shrill note on my whistle. The end word on each of my commands came out almost as a bark and would have done justice to any sergeant major as I stood before that little army of children. Most of the boys wore hobnailed boots made of stiff leather and it could not have been an easy task going through all that compulsory drill, but everybody seemed to enjoy it and more often than not returned to the classroom rosy-cheeked and ready to get on with the next lesson which was always arithmetic.

School dinners were not provided and as most children lived too far away to go home for a meal, they arrived each morning with an assortment of food for me to warm. I had been haunted by black coal ranges all my days and sure enough it was in my classroom that one of these monsters was situated, as well as a sink in which to wash the dishes with hot water drawn fro a large urn on top of the stove.

I never saw such an assortment of pasties in my whole life, some large, some small, some nicely browned and others so anaemic-looking that they appeared never to have been baked at all. First thing in the morning the pasties were placed on a large table, all suitably marked and ready for me to put in the oven at the appropriate time, usually between the two lessons that followed morning break.

Some children brought cottage pies, others ordinary pies, while others brought along eggs occasionally which were a real headache to me. What with two shelves of pasties to warm without burning them, pies bubbling over on the stove and then,

"I want my egg done 'ard," or, "Please, I want mine runny," on top of everything else, it was enough to make me want to turn my back on top of everything teaching forever. Often, in the middle of a lesson I had to dash to the oven because I could smell the pasties burning and on one unforgettable occasion I even allowed the whole lot to burn almost to a cinder.

My classroom was also the dining room and just after twelve o'clock when the children were all seated around the long tables the Head Teacher arrived to give out the various items of food. With so many pasties to identify it was no wonder in the middle of the exercise a voice would ring out over the hubbub,

"Please sir, I've got the wrong pasty," only to find that someone had taken great bites out of the right one! Hurrah for the school meals service of today. I do not think many pupils or their teachers realize how lucky they are in this respect.

The range was a black devil and once I nearly caught the school on fire when I was trying to make some earth perfectly dry as an experiment I was preparing for a nature study lesson. I had thoughtlessly placed the damp earth on a sheet of newspaper in the oven and then forgotten all about it. My colleagues and I were in another room while the children were playing outside in the playground during the dinner hour when suddenly there was a terrible commotion. Someone had noticed flames coming out of the oven door that I had left slightly ajar. The head was their frantically dealing with the situation when I arrived, red-faced, on the scene and he clearly thought he had a first class idiot on his staff. Apparently there were no words that would adequately fit the occasion. He just let out a "Grrrr," and left me standing.

However, in spite of this fall from grace the Head soon discovered that nature study was among my favourite subjects and yet I had been such a duffer at it when a schoolgirl. He suggested that I should take the senior class once a week for this subject while he would take my class for reading.

Discipline was such in the school that though some of the senior boys were like young Tarzans and very rough indeed, not one of them ever dared to play up during the lessons. I was not very much older than some of them and they could easily have wiped the floor with me but instead they listened attentively to all I had to say and made suitable notes and drawings afterwards without a murmur.

You would not have thought that these country teenagers would have been the slightest bit interested in the life style of such creatures as snails, worms and lizards but they appeared to lap it up and took great pride in their note books. But this was all before television and I would not have been able to compete with the wonderful natural history films that children are now able to watch in schools as well as in their own homes and are so educational. T.V. does after all have some good points....

I never once saw the Head Master use the cane, which he kept in a cupboard for just one word from him was enough. His name was Goodman, a very appropriate name indeed for this he was in every sense of the word. The children knew how far they could go and in such a small school nobody was likely to get away with any misdemeanour. It was the same for the teaching staff. No lack of effort would go unnoticed and we were all kept on our toes knowing that head teachers were well acquainted with everything that went on in their classrooms.

During the first two years that I spent at the school, lessons had to be prepared, written out and then presented to the Head for his approval. A detailed record of work actually done by the children was expected to be kept for his reference at any time. During the year I was on probation, he would often pop into my classroom to observe my teaching methods and I would always hate it if he found me in the middle of talking to the children for I was extremely nervous and the words just tumbled out of my mouth unnaturally while more often than not I found myself blushing to the roots of my hair.

However, after twelve months at the school I had apparently proved my practical proficiency as a teacher to the Board of Education, for following the visit of one of His Majesty's Inspectors I received the certificate that finally established my competence as an uncertificated teacher. Strange that! I was awarded a certificate but was labelled 'uncertificated'. It is a good thing that I kept that small piece of paper for it was to prove a very valuable document indeed.

The inspector stayed all day in the school and we had not been warned of his proposed visit, so he saw the three of us as we really were. How different nowadays. Inspectors rarely call unexpectedly and so everybody is able to put on a show on that particular day even if a bit slack on other occasions! I always felt terrified of HMI's even though they were quite human really and were not always looking for faults. Indeed some of them were prepared to make allowances for inexperience as illustrated by one inspector who told of a visit he made to a classroom where the teacher was not doing very well. He felt sorry for her as she had a difficult class and she was an appealing little thing. He did not think he could right her off completely so got over it by writing in his report, quite truthfully, 'Miss --- is a pretty fair teacher.'

That was his version anyway....

Chapter 23

I stayed at Otterham for three years but could not have endured it had I not been able to go home at weekends. There was nothing wrong with the school and I loved the children: it was just that living in such an isolated place was one big yawn.   There was nowhere to go when I got home from school; in the winter especially, it was always the same routine.

There was a wireless set in the bungalow but it was rarely used except for the news and I missed the lighter programmed I enjoyed so much at home. My brother had built a radiogram out of bits and pieces and though it left a great deal to be desired, it served us well.

Now that I was working, I could afford an occasional record and the Big Bands of the day were very popular with my brother and me. Henry Hall, Harry Roy and Jack Payne were great favourites at the time and we played our records over and over again. My favourite songs were "When the Poppies Bloom Again' and 'Chapel in the Moonlight' and even in those days there was a list of top tunes printed in the newspapers.

When you are 'in digs' and living as one of the family you cannot turn on the wireless just when you feel like it and anyway the landlady was very narrow minded and the sound of dance band music in her household was unthinkable. Occasionally you could listen to 'Monday Night at Eight' but that was a very rare treat.

The only thing I really remember listening to on that seldom used wireless set was the abdication speech of Edward the Eighth and while I in my girlish romanticism had a lump in my throat at the sadness of his words, it was clear what my landlady thought about the whole affair,
"Good riddance!" she said righteously, "I always knew he was a misfit."

Naturally I looked forward to the weekends when even our small town seemed to be a very lively place indeed after the humdrum routine of life at Otterham. My mother said that Launceston was the last place God made and then he never finished it, but it drew me like a magnet every Friday evening.

The train fare home was half-a-crown. It was amazing that there was a railway station in a town so small and remote a place as Otterham but it served a wide area. Sometimes I swear there were only two passengers on the train as it bore me home to freedom. Occasionally I found myself in a carriage with dear old Murrumbidgee on her way home from her Friday evening teaching stint at Camelford. Only a few teachers had cars and she must have 'trained it' for many years.

I soon found out that the train fare made too big a dent in my income. I earned just over seven pounds a month and was always waiting for payday. I paid my landlady fifteen shillings weekly and my mother five shillings, leaving me with less than a pound for the rest of each week. A month seemed interminable especially when five Fridays loomed on the calendar.

I had acquired a bicycle during the summer holiday which I paid for by installments and this was to save me many a half-crown for to help stretch my salary, I decided to cycle the sixteen miles to and from my mother's newly acquired flat in the centre of town.

The journey over the moors was quite pleasant in the spring and summer but very daunting in wintertime. However, on a good day with the wind in my back I could do the trip in less than an hour. It was fine going home but getting up early on a Monday morning facing a sixteen mile ride to work seemed grim indeed. Sometimes I cycled home mid-week especially if there was something good at the cinema. On one occasion I rode the sixteen miles in pouring rain to see a George Formby film and sat in the front row of the crowded hall with my clothes almost steaming. It was completely mad but I reckoned it was well worth it for it relieved the monotony of my life and was a good laugh although on the whole I was not very fond of funny films.

Fortunately I did not have to cycle home every weekend. The Headteacher had a small car and occasionally took his wife home to visit her parents in Launceston and then he would offer me a lift both ways. It was always a blessed relief when I could leave my bicycle in the shed and enjoy the luxury of being driven over the miles instead of pedalling like mad and battling against the elements. With so much cycling my skirts were always out of shape and it probably accounts for the fact that I became very much the shape of a pear!

There was something else too which helped mew through the three years of isolated existence. After five years of mooning over my indifferent boyfriend, I was at last able to shrug him out of my life altogether. Up until now it had always been me who got 'the brush off' and 'I Never Had A Chance' was very much my theme song. Now, however, it was a different story and the word s of the current song 'You Turned The Tables On Me' were appropriate as far as he was concerned....

****

On the other side of town, quite unknown to me throughout my years as a schoolgirl, lived a boy whose life had been almost a duplicate of my own. He too had won his way to grammar school but being one of eight children and fatherless like myself, he knew what it was to go without.

He had gained his school certificate at sixteen and as any further education was out of the question went to work as a counter assistant in a chemist's shop where his wages were exactly the same as those which had been offered to me at the grocer's. He was three years older than I so that at the time that I was desperately seeking work he was already earning a few shillings a week.

He had seen me regularly passing the chemist's shop carrying the boxes containing the teachers' washing and wondered vaguely where I could be taking all those flowers that he imagined those boxes must have contained. I had always carried them so carefully, held flat and to his mind this could be the only explanation.

Later on, after I had left school and occasionally called at the shop for soap I had thought him a very nice young man and liked the way he handed me my purchases with the words, "Three pence, Miss. Thank you," but that he could have been the slightest bit interested in me at the time never entered my head. After all he was walking out with a very pretty girl from the draper's shop next door and it was only long afterwards that I discovered that in his mind I had been 'his little soap girl' and that he had been well-aware of the similarities in our lives.

Towards the end of his apprenticeship it was suggested that he should go in for Pharmacy and train for the necessary qualifications but his mother could not afford it and so he, like me, had tried to get into the Civil Service. Like me, he failed the examination and then had to find work, which would take him off his mother's hands. He settled for the navy, took the entrance exam and at the time he took the first step right into my life was in the Supply Branch and looking very dashing indeed in his peaked cap and navy blue uniform.

So there we were with almost perfect matching lives, both slightly scarred by our experiences of hardship but now on our own feet at last and drawn together by the common denominator of circumstances. I reckon he knew what he was doing. I had had a good education and would be able to write him long letters when he was overseas and it was unlikely that anybody would steal me from him! It was certain that he did not fall for my looks for according to him I had mousey hair, frog's eyes, rabbit's teeth, a pigeon chest and suffered from 'duck's disease'. Nevertheless he considered that I was 'the cat's whiskers so what better compliment?

And so it was that my life at Otterham was made a little more bearable at first being able to meet during the weekends when we were both in Launceston and then, when he went abroad, having letters to write which passed many a long evening.

He was away for three years and two months with only one short break of a few days just before war was declared and he had to go back again without completing his leave. All that time apart! It is almost a lifetime when you are young but his letters helped me along and as I followed his voyage on the map during peacetime at least, I learned more geography than I had ever done at school.

It was not my intention when planning this book to make it a love story of the usual kind so I do not now propose to go into the details of that lovely romance. It had its ups and downs of course, even by post, for everybody knows that true love never runs smoothly, but it triumphed in the end and we forged a happy life together.

Sufficient to say that having survived that first long separation we got married during the war, eventually had two children, a boy and a girl and built a very happy family. We came through many inevitable long separations when I faced the added anxiety of his safety at sea, and even the time spent together when he was home based often came abruptly and agonisingly to an end because of further overseas draftings.

We watched The Battle of Britain from the back garden of the house where we had rooms on the east coast and our daughter was born while the bombed rained on London, not far away. My mother wrote and begged me to come home, away from the danger, but the time we had together was likely to be very short and when you are young and in love what do a few bombs matter?

The lonely time I had spent at Otterham seemed never to have happened, as did the two years I spent teaching in Camelford prior to my marriage. We had been just about to start a new term when war was declared and we all started walking about with our gas masks slung over our shoulders and wondering where it would all end.

The little town had been overflowing with evacuees and the number in my class of juniors increased to forty-one. I had been teaching for only five years when I finally left to join my new husband on the east coast. He had come home safely from the Battle of the River Plate and I was going to be with him for a few precious months anyway.

In today's language I was really and truly living on 'Cloud Nine' and I never gave school another thought.

Not for some time, anyway.

Chapter 24

At last the war came to an end and my Chief Petty Officer husband who had by then completed his twelve years in the Navy decided to take his chances in Civvy Street. He had no clue as to what he would do now to earn a living but eventually decided to have another go at the Civil Service Examination. This time he was successful.

In the meantime he had been offered a post in the town with the Health Service and after seven years of living in rooms and sharing a kitchen we had actually got a home of our own at long last. The Civil Service offered a secure future but it would mean uprooting ourselves yet again so we decided to stay put in Launceston where everybody knew nearly everybody else and we never once regretted that decision for our roots went deep and wide.

In an emergency I occasionally helped out with some teaching in the local schools but Fate had decreed that now was the time for me to repay the debt I owed to the woman who had set me on a course when I had been a schoolgirl.

One day in 1948 I was helping out with clerical duties in the District Education Office when T.A. walked in and saw me banging away on the typewriter.

"I wish you could come and help me," she said wistfully, "There is so much to do in school these days. I don't know which way to turn." Horwell Grammar School for Girls no longer took fee-paying pupils - a big step forward - but it seemed that the successful future of young people at that time depended on the passing of the Eleven Plus Examination. More anxious parents and still more anxious pupils! But that was by the way as far as I was concerned and the education scene was drawing me back once more.

I could think of nowhere I would rather be. It would be wonderful to go back to my old school again and take up the duties I had carried out as a girl so many years ago, but when

I told T.A. that I would be delighted to give her a hand I had no idea that things would move so swiftly.

It was arranged that I would work at the school for two hours in the morning and two in the afternoon and actually get paid for doing so! The pay was two shillings an hour which T.A. considered to be an insult, but it was the County Rate and I had no complaints for I would once more be getting back into the school environment which I loved so much and at the same time trying to settle an outstanding debt of gratitude.

It is strange how things work out. T.A. was nearing the end of her teaching career and no wonder she did not know which way to turn. Administration duties had multiplied considerably since my young days what with school meals, school milk and travel facilities for the long distance pupils on top of everything else and there were no school secretaries. I considered it a privilege to be one who, for the next five years, was able to make things a little easier for the woman who had done so much for me.

She had trained me well in the earlier years and it was easy for me to take over the extra jobs that had been gradually getting her down. I was in charge of requisition orders and deliveries, dinner registers, milk forms and numerous other everyday clerical tasks. And the other teachers welcomed me too for I always typed the end of term examination papers for the whole school thus relieving them of this extra work.

Three of the old stalwarts were still at the school, the teachers who had once despaired of me ever passing examinations, and now there was I helping them and always referred to as the secretary though I was, according to my time sheet merely a 'clerical helper'. It is interesting that for the whole of the seven years I acted as school secretary my wages never changed, being always two shillings an hour and no holiday pay. But that did not matter; prices were stable then and I had a husband to support me. I loved being at the school and when T.A. finally retired I stayed on to help the new Headmistress who followed her and became a very good friend to me.

There is no doubt that 'school' seemed to be a place where I was meant to be and both Heads were always telling me how helpful I was to them. The only prize I had ever had at school was inscribed 'For General Helpfulness' but I regret that I had never taken kindly to helping in the home, only at school; a sore point indeed between my mother and myself when I was a schoolgirl.

T.A. eventually left the town but we corresponded regularly and when she died I was proud to be the only one of the many pupils who had passed through her hands who was invited to attend the private funeral. She had been more than a friend to me really and I hope that in some measure I repaid what I owed her.

It was while I was working at Horwell in 1950, that both Granny and Auntie Min died. There had been a wonderful family get-together for Granny's hundredth birthday the previous year and I had been able to arrange for messages of congratulations for both old ladies in the BBC 'Family Favourites' programme compered by Franklyn Englemann. The record chosen was 'The Better Land' sung by the Kentucky Minstrels and so appropriate in their case. What would I have done without them? They were fairy godmothers indeed but there was no way I could repay them in the same manner that it had worked out in T.A.'s case. Perhaps going to see them was enough? They both enjoyed 'family' and the simple things in life. There were always children around them and being presented with grandchildren must have given the both great pleasure, for there is no doubt that as they came along they were Minnie's great-grandchildren as well as Granny's. They would very likely have considered all this payment indeed for all they did together to see us through.

****

It is thanks to T.A. I am sure that I developed such a love of words that even a dictionary was a book I liked to pick up and study. She had been my English teacher throughout my school career and there is no doubt that hers was my favourite subject. I was fascinated by the use of language and it was inevitable that my main hobby would be of the literary kind.

During the war when my husband was far away I became interested in the 'Bullets' competition run for many years in the weekly magazine, 'John Bull'. Briefly, it was a case of thinking out endings to any of the phrases that were listed each week using no more than four or five words to say something witty or with depth of meaning. These 'mental gems of the mind' as they were sometimes called, were known as 'Bullets', for it was Shakespeare himself who wrote of 'these paper bullets of the brain' and that is what they were.

The people who entered these competitions were real addicts as a rule and I was no exception. Every week I sent off my lines to London accompanied by the entry fee which was never more than a shilling in my case, and then waited optimistically for the 'Joy Wire' which the telegram was known as, which always came each week to notify the winner that one of the lines submitted had won first prize.

Except for a lean period during the war when there were fewer entries, the prizes were enormous and sometimes, as well as the lump sum offered, a pension for life was added or other 'plus' items such as luxury kitchens and overseas travel. One of the biggest prizes ever offered in the competition went to a competitor who wrote: For Services Rendered - King 'Pinned on Cross'. It had a superb double meaning and was considered to be the classic Bullet of all time.

I was determined to reach the top too for the competition was such that to be the author of the best line in anyone week was such an achievement in itself that the actual prize seemed almost to take second place. I entered the competition regularly for five years with little success but I received many 'Good Shot' acknowledgements that were encouraging and I enjoyed browsing over the winning lines and reading about the people who had won big prizes. I spent hours poring over the lines people had written over very many years, even those before I had ever heard of the competition, and I spent so much time trying to construct my own lives that my mother declared it would 'turn my brain'.

Then, in 1947, I wrote my first successful line. I must have been thinking about all the people who had been kind to me in my life and it ran: 'Key to Peace Of Mind - Kind Find'. For this I received the second prize of £25 and a holiday for two in

Wales. It was then that I met other prizewinners and actually held a Joy Wire in my hand. It had been received by a coal miner who was an addict like myself and was enjoying this holiday with his son as part of his prize. He had already won two first prizes, one including a pension of two pounds a week for life and he was using his prize money to help send his two sons to university. One of his winning lines was, 'Happier World - Or Chuckling Baby Betrayed'.

More than ever my main ambition in life was to capture a first prize for myself but it took until 1951 when I nearly died of shock as a result! I had imagined it happening for so long that when 'Telegram Tim' as he was called by regular competitors called at our door holding the coveted greetings telegram in his hand, I just couldn't believe it was happening to me and was in a state of collapse.... I had won £500 plus a luxury European coach tour for two. The words given in the list were simply, 'The Usual - ' and I had added just five words of my own, which, not counting the holiday worked out at £100 per word. I was over the moon with joy for I had got there at last and with little money behind us, the cheque would be very useful indeed. Several of my friends could not understand what I had written. They said the competition was all double Dutch anyway but my own line seemed perfectly simple to me and perfectly summed up the state of the world as it was then, is now and probably ever will be,

'The Usual Mistakes - Reason Man's Facing Wall'.

I had drawn on my schoolroom experiences and saw mankind facing a 'wall' of trouble and, as well, metaphorically speaking 'in disgrace' like a small child being punished for persistently making the same mistakes and being made to face the wall. And the worst mistakes of all as far as I could see when it came to world affairs were fear and mistrust.

The tour of Europe was an unforgettable experience and it seemed impossible that it was I sailing along with my husband in a gondola, going to the top of a mountain in Switzerland and walking regally down marble staircases in the magnificent hotels, which accommodated us. It was all like a dream and when we came home I still could not believe that it was I in London and giving a talk to several other prizewinners about our travels. But it must have happened for I have the photographs to prove it as well as the detailed account I wrote describing all that happened.

I had many successes during the following years and each one was drawn from my own experiences of life. I thought of Granny as I wrote, 'Makes Us Offer - Of Peace Within - Church' and of my own happy marriage when I offered, "Makes Her Home Ideal - EVERTHING Money Can't Buy.' Then later on when my son was on his way, 'Approaching

Motherhood - Wishing WORLD Would Knit'. The last two were written for another competition after the magazine 'John Bull' was no longer published and thousands of us had to find another, similar contest to fill the gap on our lives. This other competition was called 'Quads' and involved the use of four words only. The first prize I won in this was,

'The Christian Label - Doesn't Guarantee What's Inside'. The prizes offered here were comparatively very small indeed and I received only a few pounds for that one which only goes to prove that once bitten by the bug, one carried on irrespective of any huge monetary awards.

Sadly, the advent of television put paid to competitions of this kind having the same magnetism but the friendliness they generated was incredible and I have many letters and cards from people who shared my love of the competitions.

One memorable line was, 'Everything We Hold Dear - In 'Undervalued' Teacher's Hands'.

It was written at a time when teachers were poorly paid but the words that attracted me were, 'Everything we hold dear' ... and in the years to come I made that phrase the basis of my whole approach to teaching.

I made no conscious effort myself to go back to the classroom; I simply drifted into it, the consequence of which I could not then have possibly imagined. It was as if it had all been mapped out for me....

Chapter 25

It was 1959 and I had done no teaching for eleven years. Meanwhile, my old school friend Grace with whom I had shared so many ups and downs had become fully qualified as a teacher and held a post at the school where I had once trembled at the wrath of the Head.

I had heard that Grace was ill and not likely to be able to work for some time but it was a surprise when I was asked if I would go and take over her class of infants. There was a different Headteacher now and he had been trying desperately to get a temporary teacher to no avail so I, having been so long out of teaching, was obviously the last resort.

Our daughter, Andrea, a pupil at the girls' grammar school had just been accepted at a training college in Liverpool; she hoped to specialise in P.E., a very far cry indeed from my own P.T. experiences in the playground at Otterham such a long time ago. Our son, thirteen years younger, had not yet started school so how could I help out in these circumstances? Michael was the reason I had left my clerical duties at Horwell and was just another of those miracles in my life. That I could have provided my husband with a SON was just incredible even though my mother had declared that it was 'disgusting' having a baby at my time of life! And I was only thirty-seven....

But that is by the way. As I said, it all appeared to be mapped out in my favour. I did not want to leave Michael in the care of anyone else so it was suggested that I could perhaps take him to school with me and keep him in the classroom where I would be able to keep an eye on him along with all my other charges.

He was longing to go to school and would not normally be admitted until he was five in a few months' time and he needed no persuasion to join me in my new venture. As it happened, Grace returned sooner than expected and the special arrangement did not last long, but it was just long enough to make me want to carry on 'helping out' which was becoming the pattern of my life.

Grace, never wanting to be away from school a day longer than necessary, had come back too soon and before long I was back with her class again, and then again. But by now Michael had been admitted to the school on top of Windmill Hill where his sister had gone and where I had been so happy as a small child.

I enjoyed the work with Grace's infants. They were very demanding for it was a large class and I was very rusty but it was a happy school and I was learning too, alongside my pupils. It was easy to see, even at the very early stage in their lives, which ones were likely to shine at school and which ones were doomed to experience learning difficulties. Some children have a flair for learning and are easy to teach while others find it difficult to assimilate even the most simple, basic skills.

Unfortunately, at that time no additional help was provided for those children that any fool could see were so desperately in need of special treatment if they were going to learn to read and write reasonably successfully. No teacher, however dedicated, could be expected to do real justice to weak 'tail enders' when there were so many other children in the same class also needing attention. And so it was in my case and my heart bled for the children I could not help in the way I would have wished.

Later on, part-time ancillary teachers were brought into the local primary schools to help with the weaker brethren and, eventually, a peripatetic service was introduced into village schools but it happened very gradually and meanwhile the number of children entering secondary school with poor reading ability was increasing.

For the next four years I was an Occasional Emergency Teacher, or at least that is what I was known as officially but I was more often in the classroom than out of it. I got quite used to going to this school and that; all the time I was adding to my experience, learning more and more about children and the different ways of teaching them.

There appeared to be no lack of equipment in the schools and it was difficult to understand why so many children seemed to be able to learn satisfactorily even when provided with so many tools for the job and working in such stimulating surroundings. And they were not at all unintelligent. There was no doubt however, that over the years children had become different beings to those I had once taught.

They were much noisier for a start and had to be told over and over again to stop talking. There was less regimentation, probably a good thing, but discipline was much more free and children were not expected to work in silence. There seemed to be a mania for 'self expression' and in my humble opinion, this over-played the idea of allowing children to do their own thing is largely responsible for the general tendency nowadays for individuals to put themselves first of all in things and never mind anyone else.

I soon became aware that on the whole formal teaching and learning were considered to be old hat and as for teaching children to read, well, those methods had certainly changed over the years. But, I was able to observe and assess each method carefully and came to the conclusion that reading at any rate had to be TAUGHT and that for many children it was never going to 'just come' as some teachers mistakenly believed.

Even handwriting, it seemed, had to be left to the children's own initiative so that they could develop their own styles and certainly they were not expected to spend much time practicing the art of penmanship from any given copy. Good handwriting was encouraged of course but unfortunately appeared to be out generally although some schools still preferred the more old-fashioned methods.

Children started school at five and left at fifteen and the first year was spent largely in 'learning the play way'. Now this was all very well for some children but not for others there was very little to be gained for in large classes there was not enough time to get around all the children and those who simply 'mucked about' were getting nowhere.

I am convinced that the sooner children get into the habit of school work the better and feel the very receptive learning between four and five could be used to better advantage. It is true that a lot of children do not take kindly to starting school and are loathe to leave their mothers' apron strings but I started at four as did all the other children at that time and though I had scores of relatives, there was not one who had a reading problem.

Michael had certainly been ready to attend school at four and liked nothing better than to sit down with books and pencils at home. He did not want to play and love learning to read and write and doing his sums. He liked to pretend he was in school even to the extent of having his milk from a third of a pint bottle, complete with straw when it was time for a break. I never forced him into any of this; he was ready to learn and I went along with it.

When he went to school as a five-year old he could already write his own name, read a simple book and add and subtract numbers up to one hundred. On his first day at Windmill he wrote out his own sums, marked them and gave himself ten out of ten! Unfortunately the teacher was not a bit pleased about this state of affairs and complained that he had had too much formal teaching at home which was why he was bored with the activities in the infants' class. According to her I had made a grave mistake.

But there were other children equally fed up with the usual classroom play between five and six; they too wanted to get on with the business of learning and were encouraged to do so at home. How could this have been a mistake when they were the ones, as well as Michael, who later passed the Eleven Plus with little trouble and went on to do well in further education?

Undoubtedly, all work and no play is not good for any child and there is a place in the school curriculum for educational play but not to the extent of holding back the pupils who need to be stretched and to the extent that some poor little souls get left behind in the noisy atmosphere of a large group of small children playing in the classroom.

It may be considered that those children who were given help at home had an advantage over the others. Well, maybe they did but I soon found out that some parents did not care two hoots about their children's education and leave it all to the teachers. Or else they plunk them in front of the idiot box and hope that this is going somehow to raise their children for them.

One mother was complaining bitterly to me that her child could not read. I did not know the boy for he was at secondary school at the time and apparently not unintelligent but he could not read the simplest of books. He was an only child, over-indulged by all accounts and a bit of a handful.

"Did you ever try to help him at home?" I asked innocently.

"Not likely," was the indignant reply, "That's the teacher's job." Well, of course it was but the help I was thinking about did not concern getting down to actually teaching the child and possibly muddling him all the more, but rather encouraging him to learn instead of giving in to his every whim.

One cannot expect small children to concentrate for long periods of time but I became more and more aware that a great many children were like grass hoppers, jumping from one thing to another and always looking for something new. Some of the children had so many toys at home that they did not play with any of them for long and soon became bored. Some had regular deliveries of comics but they could not really settle to read any of them. It was easier just to look at the pictures and even though some of them had books galore, it was only a case of skimming the contents. Not many children, even the brightest of them, seemed to go in for thoroughness any more. It was all speed!

Children were encouraged to use their imagination and the bright ones were able to do so in their compositions and other creative work. No teacher would want to stunt a child who showed talent in this direction but in some cases it was at the expense of accuracy when it came to spelling and punctuation.

"Never mind the spelling," was the general rule. "Let's have the children's ideas." Splendid! Obviously, a page of imaginative composition sprinkled with a few errors is preferable to two or three unimaginative sentences with no mistakes at all, but I could see no virtue in pages of almost illegible roving of the imagination and undoubtedly full of mistakes which, repeated often enough, could only lead to later, difficult-to-undo habits.

Much of the teaching that I observed during those four years was of excellent quality however, and I hoped that some of it at least was rubbing off on me. Such a long period in various classrooms talking to the teachers and learning so much from them seemed to me to be a better training than I would ever have experienced in a training college.

****

And then, out of the blue came the secondary modern school and the problems of the older, less able children. I had served my long apprenticeship and knew I had something to offer. My life had been such that I knew what it was like for them but although I had experienced a few pinpricks I knew that I had not suffered, really suffered, thanks to those marvellous souls who were always there when I needed them.

I had emerged as a very privileged human being for whom everything seemed to have worked out and I was not poised ready to spring into action among the less fortunate children in the classroom. What a challenge! And, what a wonderful way to enter the autumn of my life....

Chapter 26

I was not going to be alone in my endeavours for not long after I decided to stay on at Pennygillam, a new teacher was appointed and she was an expert in dealing with less able children. She was full-time while I was only part-time but between us we were able to build up a good remedial department.

Betty Miller was a strict disciplinarian and was going to stand no nonsense. She knew her job inside out and the children knew that she did. I learned more from her than from all the books I had studied in order to fit myself more exactly to the work I was doing. From these I learned all the jargon connected with remedial teaching - the dos and don'ts and the various tests that could be applied to assess levels of intelligence and ability.

My work had become an obsession for I found it all so challenging and fascinating; so much to do and all so rewarding. Betty accompanied me to the various courses designed to aid teachers like ourselves but I suspect she did not need the help herself for she was well-equipped to deal with the many aspects of the work involved. We also visited special schools designed for children with severe mental and physical disabilities and talked with the pupils and their teachers. The work that we saw made me realise how much easier our own task was, comparatively speaking, and made me feel very humble.

We had our difficult pupils too but on the whole the response to the effort we put into our work was very good indeed, I shall resist the temptation to write in full about the various methods we used, for although very interesting to me, it would probably make boring reading for anyone else so I shall concentrate on the more general aspects of what was involved.

There were on average between sixty and seventy pupils needing special help and these were divided into four year groups, giving us roughly between fifteen to eighteen pupils to deal with at any one time. The ability range was such that on entry at eleven years old, some children could not read at all while others could possibly read quite fluently but could barely add together five and five. One girl could look at the word 'cat' and laboriously sound out c---a---t and then say triumphantly, "Dog". Another, faced with the problem of adding together one and nine, would find it all too much and give up in despair. These, of course, were extreme cases and should have been in special schools but if their parents would not agree to let them go there, then there was nothing we could do about it except struggle on.

Others in the group having no such difficulties, being reasonably able, might nevertheless be suffering with emotional problems which were holding them back but whatever the problems, one needed to be very patient and ready to stand up and cheer at the smallest success and above all to communicate one's delight to the children.

Not all my work was concerned with the less able: we were very careful not to use the word 'backward'. Once a week I took a third year 'A' group of about thirty for English and this was a very pleasant experience in every way and had its humorous moments.

I had no illusion about myself and though I was still only in my forties I expect my pupils thought I was very ancient indeed.

Youngsters are like that. Anyway, we were at the Cliff Richard stage and the Beatles had arrived on the pop scene. I was a fan too but doubtless my charges would not have imagined that teachers of my age could possibly have a liking for such modern entertainment. This was brought home to me in one of my lessons when I was going over with them the compositions they had written about who they would most like to meet.

Almost every one of the girls had chosen Cliff Richard and I remarked that while I understood very well the choice they had made, it would have been nice to read about somebody different for a change.

"Who would you have chosen, Miss?" one girl asked and before I could open my mouth a loud whisper came fro the back of the room where the bigger boys were sitting,

"Rudolph Valentino." Everybody laughed, including me for I was on good terms with my pupils and with the boy concerned in particular. Like Betty, I too was a strict disciplinarian but I don't think any of the pupils regarded me as a Mrs. Bossy Breeches. We were all good friends and worked happily together. There is something to be said for a few grey hairs I am sure since they tend to give the children the feeling that the teacher has lived long enough to know what she is talking about.

I have seen some young teachers who, in an effort to get on the right side of their pupils, have allowed them to become too familiar and have ended up with near riots I their classrooms. Children certainly do not like to be bossed around but they do, I feel sure, like to feel that there is someone in charge who is in command of the situation. They have little respect for a teacher who lets them do just what they like, whenever they like.

Anyway we had a good laugh over Valentino and I told them I was surprised that they had even heard of him since he had been on the scene so very long ago but I felt bound to add that I wouldn't have wanted to meet him as he was too much of a 'smoothie' and I like honest to goodness country types. They still wanted to know whom I'd like to meet, however, so I settled for Gary Cooper and left it at that!

The children in this group were a joy to teach and I looked forward to the hour I spent with them each week working on their written English. Some of the less able children wrote entertaining compositions too, like the one in which I read, 'My mother has straight hair and a very curly bottom' while another wrote, 'Our teacher has frilly teeth'. How observant children are in some respects, yet in others they seem to go around with their eyes shut. According to my husband I had rabbit's teeth because they were notched along the bottom. How much nicer to read that they were 'frilly'. I liked that.

To think that when I had first come to the school I was longing to be relieved of my duties, yet once having made the decision to stay I could not have imagined myself so totally committed anywhere else. Maybe it was because I had Betty to lean on for she bore the brunt of most of the senior work and was a tower of strength.

Meanwhile, big changes were in the offing. The girls' grammar school had merged with Launceston College in 1962 and catered for all the boys and girls who had passed the Eleven Plus exam and although everyone had thought that the Secondary Modern pupils would eventually be housed in a brand new building of their own, the decision was made in 1965 to go 'Comprehensive'. It had happened in other districts so we all knew what was involved while we waited for the necessary large extensions to be built on to Launceston College, making one big school for the whole area.

The two schools now to be merged were about half a mile apart so that for almost two years there was a great deal of pupil and teacher exchange with which to contend. The Headmaster of the College, Mr. DF Rowe, M.A., was now in charge and I will always be grateful to him for the change that he eventually brought in to the lives of the struggling slow learners. They were no longer housed on the perimeter of the school but brought right into the centre of things and provided with one of the more attractive rooms on the site.

In order to make administration more bearable during the last year before moving into the new buildings, our site became the junior school while the newer buildings further along the road housed the seniors. There was no longer an Eleven Plus exam so everyone started off on an equal footing, taking the rough with the smooth under present circumstances. This meant that Betty had to leave us for most of the time and take up her duties with the third and fourth year pupils in the college sector. It was a wrench but we still worked together as a team and I was left with the younger pupils in my own base with no more hopping about from one classroom to another.

It all seemed to be too good to be true for every afternoon for almost two terms I let myself into my own classroom with my own key and worked happily with my special children. The, wham! It seemed that it was all going to come to an end....

****

The total number of pupils in the now one school was such that the half of a teacher I represented could be replaced by a full-time one and it looked as if I was on my way OUT.

I was heart-broken. How could I leave these children and the work that meant so much to me? I had no thought of applying for the full-tie post for I felt sure the new Headmaster would not want me on his staff. There were so many of his teachers with degrees and I had heard it said that as he was a new broom, he would only want to keep teachers with the highest qualifications. And there was I who could only claim to be uncertificated and still one of the lesser breed. Was I ever going to be good enough?

Time went by, the new post was advertised and I felt like a pricked balloon. I had worked out my own reading scheme that was proving very successful indeed and Betty said it would be a waste if I gave it all up now. I still did not feel I wanted to commit myself to full-time teaching; after all, even part-time work had left me drained by the end of the day and anyway, if the truth be told, I felt that I could not possibly face rejection should I apply for the post and then be turned down. I just could not bear to think of it.

I had completed almost five years of doing the sort of work, which suited me perfectly and had been on the teaching scene over a period of nine years. I did not know how I could face giving it all up. I looked around the classroom and saw the fruits of my labours. The children were all making progress. They were happy, their parents were happy and I could go on being happy, according to Betty. But I <u>must</u> apply for the post. It was no good feeling sorry for myself and doing nothing about it.

After much thought and inner turmoil my application went in and I could neither eat nor sleep. I could see no further than the end of the summer term when the new school would be ready and I would be out on my heels, rejected and dejected.

But another miracle was about to happen and the day came when the Chairman of Governors was telling me that I had been chosen from the four interviewed candidates to take over the full-tie remedial teaching of the juniors in the new school. The other three candidates had splendid qualifications but lacked experience with slow learners and without doubt if someone like Betty Miller had applied I would have stood no chance whatsoever. Fate had smiled on me once more.

I sat before the Chairman of Governors in the Headmaster's study in a daze with my legs like jelly.
"We have decided to offer you the post," he said. "Will you accept it?" There was a three-cornered lump in my throat and

I could barely speak. I forget what I said by way of acceptance but then he was talking about salary. He explained that as I was not a fully qualified teacher I could only be paid at the starting rate of a teacher just out of college and my years of experience could not count as being of any incremental value.

What did I care about that? All I wanted was to carry on with my work. Obviously the new set-up would be a severe test after only part-time work but I had come to the conclusion that I worked best under pressure. I was fifty years old and still only a 'beginner' but I was determined to prove that I was good enough and this became the driving force behind everything I did in the years that followed. I had to show that, qualified or not, I could do the job as well as anybody else....

I left the study on unsteady legs with the Chairman's words ringing in my ears,
"We know that you do not want this post just for the money. You love your work and we wish you every success."

I slipped away into the cloakroom and had a good cry.

Chapter 27

I was riding high, on the crest of a wave, when suddenly, halfway through the summer term, Betty took the wind out of my sails and told us that for personal reasons she had to leave us. There was no time now to appoint a permanent replacement ready for September so this meant that I would be responsible for setting up the Remedial Department in the new building. It was a terrible blow and presented me now with yet another challenge. It was certainly something for me to get my teeth into and there was much planning to do.

Firstly I made arrangements to attend a course for teachers of slow learners at St Gabriel's College in London. This was to last for most of the summer holiday and proved to be very helpful indeed. The lecturer had a handicapped child of his own and therefore had more than usual interest in the education of such children. He was very experienced in the work and really put us through our paces but the times when the group got together informally exchanging classroom experiences and ideas with each other were of even greater value than the actual coursework.

It was during one of these get-togethers over coffee that I should have gained some of the self-confidence that sadly always seemed to elude me. We were talking about the teaching of reading and as it had long been a favourite topic of conversation of mine I was really letting myself go, even to the extent of thumping the table. Afterwards a Headmaster told me that he had been impressed with my enthusiasm and asked if I'd consider coming to teach in his school. I looked at him in astonishment and explained that I already had a post and anyway I had my family to consider but he outlined the various ways that he could help me overcome my difficulties, even to the extent of providing a job for my husband as well. Of course, I could have told him I had no qualifications and left it at that but I let him go on thinking that I would have been the answer to his prayer for it was nice to be wanted.... But it didn't do a great deal for my self-confidence really for I decided that he must have been pretty desperate and may indeed have been the Head of a dreadful school to which no teacher would go! All the same I was beginning to see that paper qualifications weren't all the world, after all.

At the end of the course we were presented with certificates of attendance and I could not help smiling when I noted that according to that imposing looking document I received, I had successfully completed a 'Course for Backward Teachers'. One of my colleagues at school thought this was very appropriate and afterwards always referred to me as The Backward Teacher. I did not mind being labelled 'backward' as long as nobody labelled my pupils thus. I hated the sort of labels, which were so hurtful to them as well as their parents.

The course had given me much on which to build so for the remainder of the holiday I busied myself making various pieces of apparatus for my new classroom and planning how I would meet the sterner challenges of full-time teaching. The lecturer at St Gabriel's College had said that a remedial teacher should never be afraid of being labelled 'Old Fashioned' and he certainly knew what he was talking about. New methods are all very well and had a place in my scheme but I was not prepared to treat my pupils as guinea pigs, experimenting with the new fangled ideas in which I had little faith. I decided to stick to the old, well-tried methods that I had already proved to be successful and around which I had built my own particular reading and number schemes.

And I had to get across to my charges that they were important to me and that I really cared about them.

****

The move from one building to another was not easy but at least a temporary remedial teacher had been found to take over the older children so I was not going to be completely on my own. The days before school re-opened were a nightmare of sorting out furniture, unpacking boxes and parcels and generally getting things straight. Teachers were scurrying to and fro checking equipment and books and timetables. At long last we were ready to begin out first term in a fully comprehensive school all on the same site.

The new buildings were magnificent and I considered my classroom to be among the best of these. It had been purpose-built and during the years, which followed, provided a haven for the many children who came to it with their own special learning difficulties.

I remembered how nervous I had been when I first went to secondary school and could well understand the feeling of the children coming to us from small village schools when they first set foot in such a large school as Launceston College: so many classrooms, so many teachers and so many pupils thronging the corridors. It was clearly too much for some of the children and for some of the teachers too, I have no doubt.

I began my work in the new school with mixed feelings. One part of me revelled in the new surroundings and all they offered while the other part of me trembled at the thought of the responsibility I now faced. What if I should fail in my task? For some time I walked into school each day not with mere butterflies in my stomach but eagles, flapping around and churning my insides into pulp. Outwardly, I appeared cool, calm and collected and nobody could have guessed the turmoil going on inside me.

Oh yes, it was very easy for me to get inside the heads of my new charges for I knew exactly how they felt. I had been terrified when I had changed schools at their age and I had been reasonably intelligent. What if I had been unable to read sufficiently well to follow a timetable or, worse still, unable to write my own name? What if I had been an over-sized eleven-year old boy who knew he couldn't read the simplest words and was afraid the other boys would laugh at him? Wouldn't I too have burst into uncontrollable tears and then have to face the scorn of the other, less sensitive children?

There were so many children to put at their ease and as they days went by, I could forget my own nerves and concentrate on making my classroom a place of security for those timid souls who felt so lost. It was always the same at the beginning of each new school year when the new children came to us. Each batch brought its 'tremblers' but once they were able to find their way around and knew there was someone to sort things out for them, they soon settled down and began to make progress.

Some took longer than others and one frightened little boy reminded me of a tortoise. He started off with his hands over his eyes as if that would shut him off from the bewildering world in which he now found himself. No amount of persuasion could get him to uncover his face so for quite a few days he simply sat, eyes, nose and mouth covered by his damp hands and occasionally letting out long sighs of melancholy. And then, as if needing a rest from this self-inflicted boredom, he would stay away from school for a few days and then appear again, still with his face covered.

I began to despair that he would ever show himself but wondered how he could possibly want to shut himself off from all the activities that the other children were so clearly enjoying? Then, lo and behold, one eye appeared from behind those hands. Then another; he was coming out of his hibernation. We had to make him laugh.

"Look," I said excitedly, "He's got eyes. And look! They're brown eyes. And just look at that mischievous face." He was gradually uncovering his face and a smile was hovering on his lips. "Well!" I said in mock severity, "He's been having us on all the time. He's not shy at all. Look, now he's laughing!"
The other children played along with me; they were very understanding of each other's difficulties. "Come on," I coaxed, "You can't be a tortoise any longer. I've never seen a

tortoise laugh." And then we were all laughing and the barriers were broken down.

The boy was not robust and never got over his extreme nervousness but he was not unintelligent and gradually made progress in his work. I invited his mother into the classroom to see how he was getting on and this was a great boost for him. It was always a great help to those children who knew their parents were interested in what they were doing.

As time went on there were more children with more difficulties to overcome but ours was a happy classroom and it was a place where they could feel secure and rest assured that whatever task they accomplished, however small, would meet with my delighted approval.

I was very fortunate and considered myself to be the most privileged member of staff in the whole school. I had my own, well-equipped base, groups of never more than around twenty children at a time and no serious disciplinary problems. I seldom took pupils beyond the third year when they were then in the hands of the qualified remedial teacher appointed during the first term after the new school opened. I had no public examinations to think about like the other members of staff and once I had got over my initial nervous state, I became completely and happily absorbed in my work.

And, best of all, I established myself as a friend to those who lagged behind and so desperately wanted to catch up. Most of them wanted to please me, a very satisfactory state of affairs, and having got that far with the children, generally everything else fell into place.

****

Through the years there were the misfits, of course: real misfits in every sense of the word but thankfully they numbered only a few. These were the ones who were known thieves and liars and who let down all the others in the group. It was difficult to love these children but I could feel pity for them because more often than not, they were pathetic victims of circumstance. I could talk to them until the cows came home, trying to reason with them and put them on the right path and yes, even shed tears for them. I was told on more than one occasion that I "couldn't expect win 'em all," and should not allow myself to become emotionally involved. How could I possibly follow that advice?

These were the pupils who were referred to the Educational Psychologist and if they were so bad that they were eventually placed in a special school, fair enough but more often than not, they remained with us for various reasons. The Educational Psychologist could not change their home conditions. None of us could. All we could do was to try to understand their problems and go on trying to set them on the right path.

They did not all come from poor or broken homes. In the same way that there are rogue animals, there must surely be rogue children - children for whom there is no excuse really and no Educational Psychologist is going to improve their behaviour by delving into their lives trying to find excuses at all costs. It seemed to me that time spent this way is simply playing into the hands of those few pupils who just delight in being awkward.

The children who really wrung my heart were the ones who had everything stacked against them both at home and at school but they did not make this an excuse for bad behaviour. Their lives were a constant battle and I marvelled at their quiet endeavour and good humour. They trusted me to help them and I was prepared to do everything in my power to make their lives a little more bearable.

****

It appeared that not many of the children in my groups had ever been to Sunday School and those who had not, told me, quite frankly, that they did not believe in God as there was no such person. One boy went as far as to declare,

"Well if there is a God then all I can say is that he's wasting his time." Clearly some of the children were just voicing the opinions of their parents for a few said that they had never been baptized and didn't even know what the word meant. It was not up to me to sway them one way or the other but I did consider that it was up to me to provide 'guide lines' so I used to say,

"Well, if you don't feel you can believe in God, why not put another 'o' in the word and believe in 'Good'?" This was not difficult for them to understand and they agreed with me that it was as well to have something in which to believe and around which they could build their lives. As I used to point out at appropriate moments, if we all believed in 'good' the world would be a better place.

Some of my pupils however were content to go on believing in God just as they had been taught at home and in Sunday School and one second year girl whose life was certainly not easy, was moved to write,

> God is good,
> God is clever.
> Everything he does is clever.
> He made the world,
> He made each tree,

Everything so good and free.

The fruit He makes is very sweet,

He made the children,

He even made me,

And I think He made

A very good job of it.

There was no need to pity that simplicity for there was a happy child.

Chapter 28

For the most part the children were delightful, uncomplicated creatures as far as their personalities were concerned and were a joy to me. I delighted in the happy laughter that so often rang out in my classroom and welcomed into it the many parents and friends who periodically came to see us at work.

There were students too who came, interested in remedial teaching and voluntarily giving up some of their time to come and help with individual reading and number work. What a wonderful help they were for while teaching machines and tape recorders are useful, they cannot in my opinion take the place of a caring teacher giving a child individual attention. Other members of staff too were generous with their time and willingly came along to give a hand.

But nobody who came stayed long enough to get to know the children as well as I did. The work was very demanding indeed but it certainly had its compensations, not least of these being the personalities I met along the way.

Each year there was at least one outstanding personality like, for example, Freddie who was a very popular, generous and delightful boy. He was a slow learner but could always come up with a bright idea if I was faced with some problem or other. Any odd job in the classroom he could do. He could stand in front of the class and give an interesting talk or he would occasionally bring one of his 'inventions' to school and explain in his old man way that it worked. He could always fit up a less fortunate child with a pen or pencil and saw to it that my 'tools for the job' were in good order. He could show me how the tape recorder worked and how to put batteries in the word boxes - always a mystery to me. If I wanted some squeaking rats or pattering feet for dramatization of 'The Pied Piper' he could always oblige; if I wanted a storm at sea he could arrange that too. He was always original.

He enjoyed doing a piece of free writing at home each week, every one a work of art as far as he was concerned, almost indecipherable but the best he could produce and therefore worthy of praise. It would be on a piece of paper that he had folded up to make a small square and then he stapled it around the edges because it was 'a secret'. He enjoyed watching my face as I opened it up and then read about his magic car or what he preferred to call his 'bicyclette'. Sometimes he would write a few nonsense sentences and then add at the bottom, "This is folss" or, he would write about his ordinary car and ran over the Headmaster. Very gory it was, brief with a gory picture to go with it but there was no malice in it - this was Freddie being dramatic and enjoying what he was doing even though it looks at times as if he had dipped his pen in tar.

His neighbour's dog "had a bak like a razr blad" because "they don't feed it" and he once wrote at the end of his piece, "The moral of this story is...."

He had a mania for cars and keys and gadgets ... and a zest for living, striving manfully to overcome his difficulties. Before he left he presented me with a key ring that I use to this day and is a constant reminder of the boy who had clearly found the key to his own happy living.

Then there was Katie, a little 'old woman' this time with a severe learning problem. Everything she did, however, except perhaps writing, was done with gusto. She was a spluttering hen (tidying the classroom), a Jack-in-the-box (always bobbing up for attention) and a little fat piglet swimming for safety (as Robinson Crusoe in free drama). Her favourite film star was Gregory Peck but she didn't know why and I don't suppose she could remember any of his films.

She was forever losing her books but bubbled over with confidence and had a go at most things. When two or three children were around my desk for help, she would peer through the thick lens of her glasses, pushing nearer and nearer until her head invariably ended up practically on the book before me. She was shortsighted but loved to follow while the others were reading and help them if they did not know a word. She could build quite hard words UPSIDE-DOWN when somebody else was reading to me and she was waiting for attention and then would hug herself with delight at her achievement.

Sometimes, during the sessions at my desk she was oblivious to everything else but what another child was reading and in her endeavours to get close enough to the book forced everything else on my desk, towards me until there was a blockade between myself and the work in progress. Then Margie would become exasperated and say,
"Katie! Look what you're doing to poor old Miss. 'Er can't MOVE." Then she would start sputtering about putting things back where they belonged. Margie was another interesting personality but that's another story and I could write a book

about these loveable characters who brought me such pleasure.

Mostly they were slow to learn, but each year only a very few of my charges could really be described as dull personalities. Indeed, some were very intelligent and simply needed a push in the right direction. One of these was a thirteen-year old Chinese boy, a border in the school who was five years retarded in reading. He had no long been in this country and there was a great deal of catching up to do, especially in English.

He was so quick to learn that I had to discipline myself not to give him too much time at the expense of the other less intelligent children for he was a joy to teach. I always prided myself on being fair to all and having no favourites so Wong had to be fitted in when I was not busy with the others before school started, at break times and because he was so enthusiastic and receptive, during my own free periods.

he was always punctual, waiting for me outside my classroom with a wide smile on his face and with his homework well prepared. Never, in all my teaching experience, had I met such a worker. Whatever I asked him to do, he did, and more. He was a wonderful example to the other children for I do not believe he ever wasted a minute of his own time or mine but he was no prig and became very popular in the classroom, working quietly on his own.

The other children were intrigued by the Chinese writing which he lightly pencilled on the reading cards to help him remember the meaning of words and sometimes, by request, he would read aloud for their benefit as he was very good at reading with expression and not in the least bit self-conscious.

Towards the end of his course with me he undertook to read the whole of the play, 'The Brahman and the Six Judges' which we put on tape during the dinner breaks. This involved reading the parts for nine different characters, which he did with great enjoyment using a different voice for each one. I swear he ended up pronouncing the words better than his English classmates and learned in nine months much more than it took some of my pupils, to learn. But then, he was blessed with high intelligence and had a quicksilver mind backed by imagination and self-discipline.

He had clearly been used to very strict classroom discipline before he came to England for he spoke of teachers using a stick and of pupils being made to crouch for long periods if they misbehaved. He demonstrated this punishment to us one day and I could well imagine the wrath of some English parents if their children were subjected to this treatment.

Some parents, however, used to suggest to me that if their children were difficult I should "clip 'em on the ear 'ole" or, "give 'em a good thump", while others thought the Headmaster should use the cane but I have never thought this to be a good way to deal with misbehaviour. It is often the case that really difficult children have had enough violent punishment at home and it has not made them any better behaved. If a boy gets the buckle strap at home and then nurses a bitter hatred to the wielder of that strap, it certainly is not going to do any good inflicting similar punishment at school. Sadly, there are some people who think that the cane is the answer to all disciplinary problems but I am convinced that had I laid a finger on any one of my pupils, or indeed if I had made them crouch, that would have been the end of our good relationship.

****

Sometimes the Headmaster came along to see us and to talk with the children. I wish he could have seen them as they really were but I knew how they felt in the presence of, as it were, The King. Somehow, in an endeavour to be on their best behaviour in his presence, they dried up and were certainly not themselves.

One day he asked me if we ever wrote and poetry, to which I replied that of course if any of the children showed any talent in that direction they had all my encouragement. I had to admit, however, that I would be lucky if I got even a well-written sentence out of some of them, let alone poetry.

But his enquiry gave me an idea. We would write a poem together, each contributing by writing one sentence on a given subject. It happened that we were experiencing a very early springtime so we walked in the beautiful school grounds to get some inspiration and then came back into the classroom and talked about what we had seen and heard. Several words were put on the blackboard and then the children were invited to write down one thought or sentence that we would all read together afterwards.

Some of the sentences we good and others incredibly bad; some well-constructed, others not but sometimes even a badly constructed sentence contained a beautiful thought and we eventually put them together and came up with a presentable, if not brilliant, piece:

Spring in winter
A few clouds race across the sky
And the sun shines brightly.
Daffodils are nodding their heads

As if to say, 'Yes it's spring'.

Pale primroses poke their faces

Through the bracken in the hedgerows.

Catkins covered with yellow pollen

Sway in the gentle breeze.

Buds unfurl, making a pattern

Against the sky.

Birds sing their love songs

And lambs frolic.

Will that VANDAL Jack Frost come one night

And spoil it all?

The children wrote it into their poetry folders in their best hand writing and drew pictures alongside which in some cases were very pleasing indeed. They had become so familiar with each other's sentences that even the very less able could recognize all the words used and it was the greatest triumph when some of them, normally only on very easy reading books and could read the poem perfectly on the tape the same as everybody else.

It had become, therefore, an exercise in original thought, handwriting, reading and speech training. And since it was read several times I hope too that it was an exercise in spelling as there was no skimming of the words, which had to be read perfectly. And, best of all, the boy who had thought out the last three lines would never have been able to write them on his own and yet, there was his idea, actually being used. It was all very satisfying and as time went by we cooperated to write other such pieces to everyone's advantage.

Summer Day

The clouds are like cotton wool

In a bright blue sky.

We walk on the daisies

Like a soft carpet.

The swallows dive and dart, searching for insects.

The sweet smell of hay

Drifts on the summer air.

Bees buzz leisurely among the flowers

Gathering honey.

Spotted foxgloves stand like sentinels

Guarding the hedges.

We walk under the trees,

Their crisp, cool leaves rustling in the breeze.

The moors look purple in the distance.

It becomes a lazy, hazy day.

Across the fields we hear

A bulldozer

Tearing up the hedges and trees making a new road.

They call it progress.

It spoils our day.

It was all based on the children's experience and some of them needed a great deal OD help in constructing their original sentences. Some could not write down what they wanted to say so the spoke their sentences into a tape recorder. Everybody wanted to take part.

I am reminded of a colleague who took his class out one beautiful day in summer and sat them on the grass, inviting them to be quiet for a few moments as they were going back to the classroom afterwards to write about what they felt.

Most of them knew what he meant but one girl wrote a composition about a worm and couldn't understand why the teacher was not pleased with her effort. As she explained to me afterwards,
"I didn't know what he was going on about, did I? There I was, sitting on the grass and it felt OK. Then I put my hand on the ground and felt a worm wriggling through, so I wrote about that. Well, he did say we had to write about what we FELT."
Such are the mysteries of the English language and the difficulties of communication.

There are so many words which have more than one meaning and so many too, which are tricky when it comes to spelling. Small wonder those children who have not mastered reading by the time they are eleven are unlikely to master the art of spelling by the time they leave school.

Chapter 29

Spelling! How frustrating it must be for those youngsters who go through their school lives knowing very well that they are hopeless at spelling. It is useless giving them a list of words to learn because they know them one day and have forgotten them the next. And spelling rules are not easy to remember either when there is so much else to think about.

Clearly, poor spelling results in many cases from the lack of reading experience and who is going to settle down and read a book while everyone else in the family is watching television? And more particularly so when reading is such hard work.

There were children in my classes who could barely keep their eyes open when I was trying so hard to teach them to read. In a few cases this was because they were on sedatives but often it was because they did not go to bed early enough. What is the matter with parents who allow their children to stay up top watch midnight horror movies or plays which are quite unsuitable? They are the parents who think or hope that teachers can perform miracles. Thankfully such very irresponsible parents were few as far as my classes were concerned, but even one or two such tired pupils can be a drag on anyone's resources and come into the category of those who cannot learn, whatever is done for them.

But, whether my pupils could spell or not, they managed to write notes to each other. They were rather more worldly than those I had encountered in my primary teaching days. One eleven-year old boy had been in the school barely a week when he wrote to a girl of the same age,
"I love you. I wud like to doo you," and another ran, "You are a dig hed and a puff. I hate you." That one was written to a boy by a boy. It was all to do with jealousy. Another time I picked up a note in the cloakroom that had been written by one of the senior boys to a girl he fancied, four letter words and all. No word of love was used and it was all so biological. What has happened to romance, I thought, especially as it was signed 'Randy Andy'!

I was responsible for the sex education of the children in my classes but I preferred to call it 'Personal relationships'. From what the children told me it was clear that many of them were very ignorant indeed when it came to the facts of life, but they thought they knew it all. They knew all the four-letter words, or most of them, and I knew that outside the classroom they swore like troopers. But in all the years I taught the slow learners, I never once heard them use foul language in the classroom. One hears it on the TV so often that it has almost become the norm to talk in such a way and I must admit that there were occasions when somebody may have been thoughtless when giving an answer, that I almost found myself saying,

"Don't be so bloody ridiculous." Such is the influence of TV.

When it came to 'Personal Relationships' I talked to the children as a mother but without the embarrassment that some parents undoubtedly feel when trying to deal with the matter. I told them the simple facts but my main theme was responsibility and caring about others. They knew that they could ask me any questions they liked and that I would do my best to answer honestly but I pointed out that even though I was married and had two children and grandchildren, I still did not know all the answers. Nobody does.

I always felt deeply moved during these sessions with my pupils and so aware of the responsibility involved as they put such trust in me. But they had their lighter moments, usually during question time when I occasionally found it difficult to keep a straight face. They all took the sessions very seriously and there were no titters or any embarrassment at anything I said.

One teenage boy was looking very puzzled and said that he had a question. He thought for a moment and then burst out, "'ow did 'em manage in prehistoric times?" I felt my mouth twitching and was ready to burst into laughter, but Stew was being very serious so I pulled myself together and began to answer his question the best I could. He still looked puzzled, however, and said,

"No, I don't mean that. What I wanted to know was 'ow did 'em manage when oxygen wad'n invented?"

Well, that really floored me. Whatever did he mean? It turned out that he had honestly believed that there was no such thing as oxygen long ago and as I had said that it was essential to the unborn baby and was provided through the umbilical cord, he wondered how mothers-to-be had managed. No wonder he was so puzzled about the whole affair and it made me all the more aware of the necessity for simplicity when dealing with youngsters such as these.

I am of the opinion that sex education is, on the whole, overdone in some cases and believe that we assume too much sophistication in the young. We often hear the complaint that children are not children anymore. Could it be that it is partly because they have been provided with too much sex instruction too soon and before many of them can really assimilate it? Do youngsters really need to see the birth of a baby on film, in full colour with all the gory details? Some of them can take it, others cannot. It is all very well talking about facing up to the realities of life - time enough for that later on when the reality is not such an assault on the mind. We protest at the violence so often seen on the television screen and yet children are exposed in school to childbirth on film and it is supposed to be helping them.

I am all for telling the children the truth as far as they want to know and it is no use tying things up in 'fancy ribbons' but there is a limit to what they need to know and there is something to be said for children being allowed to be children and able to enjoy the 'precious years'.

Unfortunately, the 'precious years' for some of my pupils were marred by the fact that they came from broken homes or had to endure the misery of living with parents who did not get on but this all the more emphasized what I tried to put across to them during my own sessions regarding personal relationships - the need to for respect and consideration for others. I did not kid myself that they would all follow the good advice I meted out but at least it was an effort to help them towards their own happier living.

****

Which brings me to my 'precious years', happy living and the love affair I was having with my work. It was all so very satisfying and the crooked lines of my life had developed into straight, purposeful strokes. Then, suddenly, out of the blue I was knocked sideways once again....

In the spring of 1970 the Head summoned me to his study and told me as kindly as he could that I was in danger of losing my job at the end of the summer term. It appeared that because of a new ruling by the Education Authority no unqualified teacher could be employed after August that year.

It was a terrible blow. I had worked so hard and now it seemed that as a reward I was going to be kicked out as not being good enough. It all seemed so unfair that I, the champion of the rejected, should now be about to be rejected myself. What a slap in the face! Talk about an inferiority complex! All through my life I had felt the need to prove myself as good as anybody else and now circumstances had caught up with me once again and the facts were clear. I was not college trained and therefore there was no longer a place for me in the classroom into which I had first drifted but now where I felt myself to be so firmly established.

The Headmaster wanted to keep me in the school and assured me that I had the backing of the Governors but the situation was such that he could not hold out much hope of me being retained. He advised me to write to the Secretary for Education in Truro and get in touch with my Union at once. The letter I received from the County Secretary was very terse and not very encouraging,

'The points you have raised are being considered and I will write to you again on this matter as soon as possible.'

And so the battle began....

I have in my writing desk a large, bulky envelope labelled, 'Case for The Defence' and it contains copies of all the letters which I wrote and those which were written to me during the following weeks. I felt like a prisoner in court fighting for me life and fearing all the time that the axe must inevitably fall.

I went about my work like one in a dream. My colleagues were as anxious as I and kept asking me if there was any news. My face must have told them the answer for it was difficult to smile under the circumstances and as I did not feel much like eating I began to lose weight as well.

There were very many other teachers in the country as well as myself facing 'the chop' as a result of the new ruling but I did have one trump card - that little piece of paper that I had kept since 1936 and which stated categorically that the Board of Education was satisfied as to my proficiency as a teacher. I had entered the teaching profession legitimately and in a manner accepted at the time and though, except for my course at St Gabriel's I had not actually been college trained, I had a great deal of experience and I felt that I was as qualified to teach as anyone.

I recognised that a fully qualified teaching service was an admirable aim but there were so many unqualified teachers at that time who had given long, satisfactory service and it seemed quite absurd to suggest that if they wanted to continue their work they should now up-sticks and go on to the required long training course.

The initial letter received from the NUT through the local secretary appealing on my behalf led me to believe that as I had once been recognised as a teacher, then I was entitled to carry on with my work, but still no word from the County Secretary confirming this. I wrote letter after letter to the NUT until the secretary dealing with my case must have been sick of the sight of my name. It seemed that I was getting nowhere though he was clearly on my side and I felt I was worrying unnecessarily.

Apparently, whether I was retained or not depended on my present status. If I came under the category of 'Occasional Teacher' then there was no hope for me at all but I knew very well that this was not the case. For a time I had been an occasional emergency teacher but then I had been <u>appointed</u> as a remedial teacher at Launceston College and had signed an agreement with the authorities. So, why couldn't someone put me out of my misery? How long before a decision could be made?

At long last, after an urgent letter of enquiry from the NUT, the Department of Science and Education made a definite ruling on my case and passed it to the County Authority. I suffered agonies of mind whilst awaiting the decision and then eventually it came ... the letter from Truro. It regretted any inconvenience caused and stated that I was, after all, entitled to teach.

I cannot describe the relief I felt at receiving the marvellous news but what heavy weather had been made of it all. As one of my colleagues remarked, it had all been a storm in a teacup. And how! Apparently a paragraph in the Circular concerning unqualified teachers had been misinterpreted and it was not until this was clarified in later correspondence received from the DES that the County Secretary felt able to make a definite decision in my case.

I could not really blame him for all the delay. Official jargon is difficult to understand and there is no doubt with so many other teachers involved it was a tricky situation but, I would not like to face those dreadful weeks all over again. My heart went out to all those long-serving teachers who had no qualifications whatsoever, not even a little piece of paper like I had, but who had nevertheless given excellent service. There was no chance that they would be allowed to carry on with their work and I knew only too well haw they were feeling.

Chapter 30

I was in full sail once more and on a straight course. There I was, doing what I liked best in the world and getting paid for doing it! Surely there was nobody as lucky as I. Over the years teachers' pay had improved and even though I was still at the bottom end of the salary scale, I considered I was well paid. Our daughter had gone through training college and became a fully qualified teacher and our son was well on his way to university. Unlike me, he had a scientific brain and was later to gain a first class honours degree in Metallurgy and Science of Materials and then a PhD, compensation indeed for our own lack of further education.

Our children suffered no hardships when it came to the financial side of things. With two parents working, they had all the advantages that we never had at their age but they were well aware of the uphill struggle it had been for both of us and never took their own good fortune for granted. We always made a point of never allowing them to have everything they wanted when they were children. Love they had in abundance but when it came to material things they were certainly not over-indulged. As a result, even though we could well afford to dip into our pockets for the extras they required for their further education, they preferred as well to help themselves along and find work during their vacations.

Andrea went egg packing and doing clerical work and Michael, in turn was a shelf-filler in a local cash and carry store, a builder's laborer and a cleaner at the library. As a schoolboy he had delivered Sunday newspapers before going on to church and provided himself with additional pocket money. I think that it is such a pity when youngsters of a certain age, given the chance of doing some paid work in their spare time are not allowed to do so by law because of the need to protect them from exploitation. There is the danger, of course, that some of them could be overworked but within limits it must be a good thing for children to earn a little money by their own efforts and not to have everything handed to them on a plate.

****

Although I was one of the older members of staff, I had always felt very much a 'junior' and was more than surprised when promotion came my way. Now that I was well and truly established as qualified to teach, I was awarded an additional allowance for my labours and then, a few years later, went up another grade to become senior mistress in the junior school. At last I was good enough.... All the same I found it difficult to believe that it was happening to me; as far as I was concerned, the senior mistress bit was just what it said, for by age I was certainly the most senior mistress in the school.

The new grade meant more responsibility of course and there were times when I found some teachers more difficult to handle than the children. But on the whole, my duties were made easier by the ready cooperation of my colleagues and the helpful advice of my superiors. The few uncooperative teachers were the ones who went on about their 'rights' but the rights they had in mind did not tie up with any sort of responsibility on their part and they provided their own unruly classes.

Some time ago I read somewhere that remedial teachers are inclined to live in a world of their own, cutting themselves off from the other members of staff and withdrawing from the usual extra school activities. This was certainly not so in my case for I enjoyed the companionship of my colleagues and the fun we shared was a relief from our labours.

My own special friend was always good for a laugh and we exchanged many a classroom anecdote. Marge taught RE among other things and was the Head of the First Year pupils so that we came in to frequent contact and shared each other's experiences. One day she had been telling her junior class about the work done by Mother Teresa in India. She spoke of the misery of the homeless, hungry and dying in the streets of Calcutta and how this wonderful woman helped them. Such human suffering made such an impression upon one boy that he was almost in tears when he declared he had heard all about it before and that it was called 'Oh-O-o-oh Calcutta'. He brought out the 'Oh' bit almost as an expression of pain and left Marge in no doubt as to his sincerity.

I wish I had kept a record of all the funny things children said to me during my years as a teacher. I always felt sure of at least one laugh a day and some incidents spring readily to mind.

In the library one day, I was trying to explain where certain sections of books were kept and asked the children if they knew what I meant by 'fiction'. Quick as a flash, one boy had his hand waving frantically in the air and answered,

"They'm special books for fick people." And he really meant it.

Another boy was at my desk confronted by the word 'church' in his reading book. He knew all the sounds and could easily have built the word without my help even if he could not get the word from the context of the sentence. But his mind had become a blank at that moment so I said "ch" and then 'ch' again.

"Come on Barrie. You know what 'ch' says. Ch -ch- ch." I was willing him to say the word. Suddenly his face brightened up and he said triumphantly, "Train!" It was at times such as these that I had to laugh or I would have burst into tears of despair.

You would think 'quick' an easy word to recognise, but the minds of some of my pupils worked in mysterious ways. Stew looked at the word on the flashcard and thought it said 'quack' and promptly said "Duck". He explained afterwards how he had come to that conclusion and then added ruefully, "What a fool!"

Sometimes I would entertain my colleagues to some mimicry of my pupils but never unkindly, I hope, and I delighted in giving them accounts of various amusing happenings in my classroom. It's a wonder they didn't tell me to dry up but perhaps they recognised that remedial teaching being such a strain emotionally, I needed to let myself go occasionally and act the goat a bit.

One tale I told was about Stevie, a very immature twelve-year old. He liked to sit up close beside me when I was reading to the class and his brown eyes, shining with excitement, would dart from the page to my face and back again as the stories unfolded and he could hardly wait to hear what happened next. He was exactly like Basil Brush when <u>he</u> was listening to a story being read, eager face and all, and soon we always referred to him as Basil, much to his delight.

One day I was on duty in the classroom when along came Basil with a decided twinkle in his eye. He nuzzled up close to me, rubbing his cheek against my jumper and then gave me a terrific nudge, enough almost to throw me off my feet.
"Boom, boom!" he said and laughed exactly like the original Basil Brush. I shall never again be able to watch that delightful bushy tailed creature on TV without thinking of Stevie and his mischievous ways.

It was he too who once called me an 'old bag' much to the horror of everyone else in the classroom. I was suitably outraged and demanded an apology but I could not blame the boy really. Life becomes too much to bear at times and frustration often leads people to say things they do not mean. And what he called me was mild compared with the behaviour teachers have to contend with in some of the schools of today. I often wonder how I would have fared in a big inner city school where, from all accounts, I may even have needed a bodyguard! Some of the pupils in our school were often difficult to handle but they were certainly not vicious and as one student once said to me, on returning from a teaching stint in London,

"It's good to be back here. After what I've been through this place is like Paradise."

All the same, my colleagues often told me that they did not know how I put up with the pupils in my charge, but it was a case of 'to each his own' for I knew that I could not have done the sort of work that they did. I take off my hat to the dedicated teachers in comprehensive schools for their work is not easy and they certainly need the holidays which sop many parents begrudge them. And when those same parents complain that their children's work has not been properly corrected do they ever stop to think how many hundreds of exercise books each subject teacher has to mark in just one week? It is a mountainous task and for some of them is just too much on top of all the other pressures brought about by comprehensive education.

I am bound to say that I am not in favour of very large comprehensive schools for to my mind they come into the same category as high-rise flats and it is a pity that either came into being. A good education is a door, which should be open to all children, clearly and a great deal, has been done in an effort to right the wrong of selective education. But, I do feel that different kinds of children need different kinds of teaching and that all ability classes in vital subjects as practiced in many schools are a glaring example of equal opportunity gone mad.

When a housewife has a load of washing to do she does not dump the whole lot into her expensive machine and hope for the best. Not if she wants satisfactory results. She first sorts out all the items to be washed and uses the correct settings for the various fabrics. And so it should be with education - the same facilities for all but with different 'settings' to suit the needs of pupils.

I wish that I were a fairy godmother so that I could wave a magic wand and provide all the money necessary for the ideal education of all. I would provide more buildings and many more teachers so that each large comprehensive school could be broken down into the smaller ones. What a wonderful transformation that would be but, alas it is only a dream which I fear is not likely to come true. Not in the present economic climate, anyway....

****

At last the time came for me to retire. I had already reached the age of sixty and although I was told that I had years of teaching left in me yet, I felt that it was time for me to go. I was very tired, not tired of teaching certainly, but physically tired. The fifteen years I had battled away were beginning to tell; I was not as tolerant as I had once been and there were times when I could easily have burst into tears. My husband too needed me at home. Through all the years of my teaching he has been a shoulder to lean on, a helpmate in every possible way. He had known so well what my work meant to me and had put up with many inconveniences at home. Now was the time for me to make it all up to him.

There was my mother too. She had reached her eightieth birthday and while still fiercely independent was beginning to rely more and more upon my visits to her small flat not far away from where we live. Now was the time to devote more time to her also and try to make up for all the sacrifices she had made in her life.

I wondered how I could bear to give up my work but gradually got used to the idea. There was now an additional teacher in the remedial department who had completed almost two years with us. She was responsible for the 'grey zone' children who were rather more able than the ones I had in my classes but yet needed extra help. She was very competent and I knew I would be leaving things in good hands.

Then, as my time to leave grew near, I began to think of my last day at school with dread, afraid that I would break down. I spoke to the Headmaster about it one day as we were having our dinner,

"Please," I said, "when the time comes for me to leave, may I be allowed to walk out of the school like on any ordinary day, with no fuss?" He did not take me seriously and simply said,

"Oh, that would be very improper." And he was right of course. Things had to be done properly.

There would be the usual presentation with speeches to go with it and I was terrified at the prospect. I could stay away from school on that day, of course.... That seemed to be a solution. But it was a coward's way out....

So, I began to consider how else I could get out of being there when school ended. I thought of myself slipping away quietly after the final assembly without saying anything to anybody. I would arrange for a record to be put on in the staff room of Frank Sinatra singing 'My Way' or perhaps Shirley Bassey singing 'This is My Life' and meanwhile would have reached home away from it all thinking of the staff tucking into the farewell spread that I would leave for them. I smiled to myself as I pictured the scene but knew that it was too 'way out' even for me, who always liked to be different.

I conjured up several farewell speeches in my mind. They were brilliant and I was going to choose one of them and put on the greatest performance of my life and surprise them all for most of them knew me as a very nervous individual. But, here again, it was only in my imagination and when the time finally came for me to go, I did the same as everybody else before me, going through the usual formalities and accepting my farewell present with a smile.

But, I was determined in the end that I would not make a speech after all. I got out of it by reading a poem instead, or rather a limerick - all very 'cultural'. I adapted one I had spotted in a magazine years before and which ran,

A teacher resigning her job,
Was heard to say with a sob,
"I'm not crying with grief,
These are tears of relief,
And I'm glad to hand over my job.

The last line originally read, "I've had more than enough of that mob" but that was not strictly true in my case and whilst it might have raised a laugh, it did not seem appropriate for the occasion.

And so I walked out of the school, not like on any ordinary day, but with the typewriter that had been presented to me, along with other smaller gifts and with the good wishes of my colleagues ringing in my ears. There was now another challenge to face - that of retirement, and I knew that was not going to be easy.

But, I had my typewriter and I had my memories so I would write my book. What better way to help fill my days and so provide my grandchildren with an insight into the way people lived, long ago.

After all, you don't <u>have </u>to be famous to write an autobiography....

Chapter 31

I am enjoying my retirement. We live in a modest bungalow on the side of Windmill Hill with all its memories and only a stone's throw away from where we had lived with my grandmother all those years ago.

The old, well-loved house was demolished some time ago in order to enlarge the Sheep Market car park but the chestnut tree around which we played as children is still there and I can just see the top of it from our kitchen window. It brings back so many happy memories.

But that is not all. As I stand at the sink washing the dishes, I can see many places that played a part in my life that it is incredible. Over there is the Norman Castle in all its majesty and the grounds where each May 24th we celebrated Empire Day and danced around the maypole.

Down there is a glimpse of the town square from which we set out excitedly on the Sunday School Outings and where I stood so reverently each November 11th, first with The Brownies and then with The Guides, honouring those who had fallen in the war.

Away in the distance at St Stephens, is the school where I first started to teach as a probationer and I can see the long hill winding up to it and the quaint houses on either side.

So near, that I can tell the time by its clock, is the tower of the church of St Mary Magdalene and what memories that brings flooding back.

There is so much to see from our kitchen window that I can pick out something different each day. There is a panoramic view of the countryside around us; the fields where I had gone blackberrying and the lanes along which I had wandered searching for daffodils and primroses. And it had been only a chance remark, which had brought us to this delightful spot to live just over five years ago, almost as if it was destined that I should spend my retirement here.

We boast that we are five minutes from everywhere that matters and that includes the Post Office where we shall soon be drawing our old age pensions! And yet, in our garden, we could almost be in the depths of the countryside. We can watch the many birds, which come to visit us, catch a glimpse of a squirrel as it scampers up a tree or even watch a family of hedgehogs by torchlight when they come for their saucer of milk.

I spend hours working in the garden and find pleasure in just pulling up the weeds or picking off dead flower heads. It is an activity that takes very little effort and is very relaxing for in the process I can allow my mind to wander at will. When I was teaching I planned out all kinds of work for the children while I was pottering in the garden - a way to help this one and a way to encourage that one....

My love of gardening was well known and I was said to be like a bee - always buzzing around the flowers and bushes. I never seemed to be anything but busy and to my teacher friends was always known as 'Bee'. It suited me very well. Busy Bee - I liked that for I hated my own Christian name and I had only one. And that is why there is no mention of it in this book.

I have so much now for which I am thankful; a husband who cares and a loving family. We have our own little bungalow, made possible by my work as a teacher and a wealth of everything that matters. A young neighbour saw me working in the garden one day and greeted me with,

"Hello. I see you're still at it then." He had been a pupil of mine at Pennygillam and stopped to talk to me as I worked. "If you had a pound note for every hour you've spent in the garden, you'd be a millionaire," he said.

It was on the tip of my tongue to tell him that to be correct, he should have made it 'millionairess' but I remembered that he was no longer in the classroom. I stopped what I was doing, straightened my back and stood up, looking for all the world like a down-and-out in my old gardening clothes.

"What do you mean?" I said with mock indignation, "I AM a millionaire!" After all, in my book it is not money that entitles one to be called a millionaire but wealth of a very different kind and I have it in abundance.

The young man went on his way with a smile on his face, and very likely not really understanding what I meant. You don't, when you are very young....

The flowerbeds were looking rather bedraggled, the wind having played havoc with the tender plants. There was much tidying up to do so I went on with the remedial work among the flowers, propping up the easily bruised blooms and helping them grow towards the sky....

Postscript
(1978)

But that is not really the end for the events of my life have turned full circle and I find myself once more a 'last resort' as in the first chapter.

On the very day that I completed this book, I was asked if I would return yet again to the teaching scene and help part-time with a few difficult boys with severe learning problems.

It had become the pattern of my life and my husband and everyone else knew what my answer would be.... I rang the Headmaster and was happy to tell him, "I'll come."

It really was as if someone, somewhere had mapped it all out for me....

Postscript

(2016)

Freda (Bee) Hicks did not retire completely until 1984.

She continued to live in the bungalow on Windmill Hill for another two decades until, widowed, she moved to Derbyshire to be nearer her son.

Today, 22nd September 2016 Freda is 100 years old. She now lives in Stratford-upon-Avon and still has a lively interest in life and a bright, active mind.

Acknowledgements

Cover Photo: Paul Harris

Photographs: pages 271 – 273 Eleanor Mason

Other photographs: Hillman family archives

Printed in Great Britain
by Amazon